Face Reading

Unlock the Secrets of Chinese Physiognomy and Discover How to Read People Like Clockwork

Your Free Gift (only available for a limited time)

Thanks for getting this book! If you want to learn more about various spirituality topics, then join Mari Silva's community and get a free guided meditation MP3 for awakening your third eye. This guided meditation mp3 is designed to open and strengthen ones third eye so you can experience a higher state of consciousness. Simply visit the link below the image to get started.

https://spiritualityspot.com/meditation

Contents

Introduction

Studying a person's face to tell if they are truthful is one of the most common ways to assess their integrity. In fact, it's a fundamental trait that most of us have without even knowing it. At the same time, we also look for concealed emotions behind a person's face, whether it's a relative, friend, or coworker.

Did you know there are ways to tell a person's emotions and decipher their luck just by reading their face? Face reading is an ancient practice in Chinese and European civilizations dating back several millennia.

If you wish to learn more about how face reading works and to try it on yourself or with others, then this book is for you. It will not only help you explore ancient alternative practices but also teach you to interpret the minds and thoughts of those around you. You can use this knowledge to better understand the people in your life, including family members, close friends, new acquaintances, or ordinary by-passers. As opposed to simply understanding the history and theoretical aspects of face reading, this book will teach you how to read faces and interpret a person's thoughts as well as their temperament.

If you are fascinated by the people you meet and want to get to know them on a deeper level (without flat-out prying), then physiognomy is a great art to learn. This book will give you a detailed history of face reading and how it works. You will learn the facial map and how to read it, complete with diagrams and step-by-step instructions. You will also learn how to decipher character traits, assess health, and read the past, present, and future of those you know, as well as those you will come to meet. By the end of this book, you are bound to see faces in a different way, with a deeper insight and compassion for the people in your life. Without further ado, let's begin our journey!

Advantages of Face Reading

While the most obvious benefit of face reading is the ability to interpret people's thoughts, several other advantages come with physiognomy, including:

· A deeper understanding and insight into people and their lives

· Compassion for others

· An eye for detail

· The ability to empathize with others

· Gratitude

The ability to read faces can significantly affect a person's life as well as their habits. Most people underestimate the amount of information that faces can reveal. How we communicate, behave, expend energy, and express our emotions are thoroughly conveyed through our faces. Along with this, your face also reveals your ability to work either independently or collectively. Moreover, your face will let others know whether you are materialistic or if you place greater value on emotions and experiences. It also shows whether you are in love, in emotional agony, had a challenging childhood, or are awaiting good fortune in the future.

So, which aspects can you hope to discover with face reading? Let's find out.

   · **Health:** A person's face is divided into "zones" (per the modern terminology) to figure out health issues in specific organs or internal parts of the body. Whether it's a nutritional deficiency, lack of physical strength, or an underlying condition, you can read a person's face to determine the precise root cause. With this, you can also resolve these issues by treating them with proper remedies, natural or otherwise.

   · **Wealth:** You can look at a person's unique facial features to grasp the amount of wealth they had in the past, what they have now, and how much they will have in the future. There are certain points on the face that tell you whether they will acquire abundant wealth through hard work or by inheriting ancestral property.

   · **Personality and Character:** You learn about a person's character, traits, and personality by reading their face. Some people can be deceptive and pretend to be someone they are not, which can make it rather difficult to discern their genuine personality. With face reading, you can look beyond the facade and understand them for who they are. Their strengths, weaknesses, needs, and behaviors will be laid bare for you to assess.

   · **Career:** By simply contemplating a person's face, you can appraise their luck, talent, and competence, which can help you advise them on their ideal career path. If you are confused about yourself, it can encourage you to choose your professional vocation as well. You can learn how to read the hidden talents and successful attributes in a person, along with their interests and shortcomings. Lastly, facial features also determine a person's ability to handle money, make connections, and lead others, which are necessary aspects of any professional environment.

· **Love and Marriage:** If you are lucky, you will meet your ideal life partner early on, but many often struggle to find the soulmate they will spend the rest of their lives with. This is when the art of face reading comes in handy. Whenever you go on a date or meet a would-be life partner, you can easily overlook their superficial features and make out their true, intrinsic self. By learning the art of face reading, you can also analyze a couple's faces and determine whether they love or are truly meant for each other.

· **Children:** The vital points on someone's face determine their luck when it comes to having kids. It also tells the health, luck, fate, and future of their offspring. Since the top part of one's face is the "Heaven" section, which represents childhood, you can easily determine the child's fate and the childhood they are destined for.

· **Destiny and Life's Purpose:** We often live according to others' expectations, which suppresses our true selves and can even result in feelings of inadequacy or self-hatred. With face reading, you get to learn what you truly want in life and define your sole purpose. For some, excelling at their work gives them ultimate satisfaction, whereas others will find solace in traveling and world exploration. With this art, you can figure out your life's real purpose and steadily achieve your goals. Likewise, you get to learn about your own destiny – what your life was and what it will evolve into. If you don't like what you read, you still have a chance to change it, giving yourself an opportunity to make amends and get reacquainted with success.

As you can see, a person's face can reveal virtually everything about them – from their childhood to how their life will be when they retire. Faces are open books ready to spill their secrets to those who master the art of face reading. Take an open-book exam as an example; you are given the liberty to consult your textbooks, notes, and cheat sheets, but if you don't know how to locate answers in the materials at your disposal, you will most likely fail the test and earn a poor grade. Similarly, a human face gives you all information; all you need is to learn the art of finding and interpreting answers, which is what this volume is all about.

In the following chapters, you will learn a great deal about the history, techniques, and approaches to effective face reading.

Chapter 1: History of Chinese Physiognomy and Face Reading

This opening section will focus on the history of face reading and its evolution through time. It is intended to give you a sound understanding of how, where, and why face reading originated and why it still exists today.

Briefly, face reading is about analyzing a person's facial features to understand their character, personality traits, strengths, weaknesses, and more. Every feature of the face – nose, eyes, mouth, lips, chin, etc. – reveals something about the person and their unique attributes. If you look carefully and learn to read facial features properly, you can unravel hidden stories, some of which could even be dark, layered secrets of their past. In addition, it also gives deep insights into a person's fate and future. In many ways, a face resembles a blueprint that lays out a person's life story, right from their childhood to their golden years. That said, it is not as easy as it sounds; you must learn how it is done and keep practicing consistently to become a master of face reading and analysis.

Aside from learning about a person's story and predicting their future, you can also determine the state of their health through face reading. This practice has endured many centuries since Taoist monk healers used the art of face reading to diagnose underlying health issues and diseases. This technique's accuracy was so remarkable that Traditional Chinese Medicine (or TCM) still employs it in medical practices today.

Before we discuss the history and significance of physiognomy, it is first important to understand what physiognomy is and what it entails.

What is Physiognomy?

Physiognomy is the art of deciphering one's character and personality through their facial expressions and outer appearance. Stemming from ancient Greek times, the term "physio" means nature, and "gnomon" means interpreter or judge. Though sometimes considered a form of pseudoscience, this technique influenced a great many scholars and teachers throughout Europe during ancient times. It is often also referred to as the art of learning about an object or terrain through specific physical attributes. For instance, physiognomy would explain the genetic connection between a person's physical traits. If someone had Down syndrome, it was apparent through their slant eyes and flat face. In time, the study of physiognomy progressed and was actively incorporated in other scientific disciplines, such as biochemistry and physiology.

Ancient Greek Physiognomy

While the study of physiognomy was exceptionally popular in European culture throughout the 18th and 19th centuries, the practice can be traced back to 500 B.C. when Pythagoras, the Greek scholar, judged his students based on their looks. If they were not "gifted" enough, he would instantly reject them. The term "physiognomonia" appeared in the fifth century B.C. in <u>Of the Epidemics</u>, a treatise written by Hippocrates. It also appeared in a scripture authored by Antisthenes, another eminent Greek philosopher.

In one historical finding, Aristotle's assessment of people's traits based on their face's size and shape further established the study of physiognomy. According to Aristotle, people who possessed broad faces were half-witted, small faces were faithful, round faces were courageous, and large heads were hostile. He also studied the noses in particular, as this body part was believed to reveal a lot about the person. The philosopher believed that people who had a sharp, pointed nose could easily be provoked, while those with a thick and bulbous one were insensitive. People with a slender and hooked nose embodied the might of an eagle, and an obtuse nose signified the courage of a lion.

In his treatise, Aristotle also clarified the approach to his study of the general and particular characteristics of the subjects' individual traits that conveyed stupidity and genius, along with strengths and weaknesses. These aspects were then studied individually and collectively to determine the outcomes. Individual features such as hair, voice, color, body, and gait were all considered.

These studies and findings slowly evolved and spread to all of Europe during the 16th century. All kinds of intellectuals, including scholars, physicians, scientists, and philosophers, set out to find the connection between a person's face and their personality and fate. Several classical Latin authors like Suetonius, Juvenal, and Pliny, the Elder drew inspiration from these studies and conducted their own research. However, in the late medieval era, these studies were more astrological than descriptive, which inspired people to use them in magic and esoteric spells.

Other European scholars also dipped their toe in the study of physiognomy and contributed their own versions to this discipline. These scholars were the most well-known figures at the time, of whom were Sir Thomas Aquinas, Avicenna, John Duns Scotus, and Albertus Magnus.

Here are the most notable works in physiognomy that date back to Ancient Greece:

· Physiognomonics by Aristotle – A book divided into two parts. The first volume focused on human behavior and how nature is aligned with the human form. The second part tackled animal nature and behavior, along with the gender roles of animals in their kingdom.

· Polemon of Laodicea, *de Physiognomonia* (2nd century), in Greek

· Adamantius the Sophist, *Physiognomonia* (4th century), in Greek

· An anonymous Latin author, *de Physiognomonia* (4th century)

Sir Thomas Browne

Sir Thomas Browne was an English physician and philosopher who influenced the discipline of physiology. In 1643, he authored a book entitled *Religio Medici*, in which he discussed the possibility of a person's inner qualities being reflected in their external appearance and facial features. In part 2:2 of the book, he writes the following:

"There is surely a Physiognomy, which those experienced and Master Mendicants observe. (...) For there are mystically in our faces certain Characters that carry in them the motto of our Souls, wherein he that cannot read A.B.C. may read our natures."

Browne also claims that the eyes and nose communicate without speaking and that the eyebrows can tell the truth. He posits that a person's individual features, complexion, and overall constitution also give away truths about them. He also coined the term "caricature" to convey political satire in visual form.

Giambattista Della Porta's work on celestial physiognomy was also a breakthrough in the discipline. The Italian scholar argues that a person's temperament was responsible for their outer appearance, not the stars as it was commonly believed. In another one of his works, he represented the human form with animal woodcuts. Browne and Della Porta concurred on the fact that a plant's roots, leaves, fruits, and structure were responsible for the effectiveness of its medicinal properties, a concept also known as the "doctrine of signatures."

John Kaspar Lavater

John Kaspar Lavater was a Swiss writer, pastor of St. Peter's Church in Zurich, and founder of physiognomics, a movement associated with religion and anti-rationalist beliefs. He was always the subject of vivid controversies, most of which related to religion. Lavater was deported to Basel in 1799 for leading an illegal protest. Upon his return to Zurich, he was injured in a fight with French soldiers, after which he died.

Given his interest in religion and "magnetic" trace conditions, he conducted several studies that he claimed could help trace and ascertain the divine energy present in all humans. He believed that the mind and body were in constant interaction, which led to the awakening of spiritual energy and its influence on a person's body. His findings can be read in *Physiognomische Fragmente zur Beförderung der Menschenkenntnis und Menschenliebe*, his most notable work, and the reason behind his notoriety.

Taoist Mien Siang Ancient Practice and Finding the Wu Xing

Mien Shiang (or Mien Xiang) is an ancient Chinese face reading art that has been in practice since 2700 B.C. during the reign of the Yellow Emperor. The art of face reading was especially significant during that era. In fact, it was deemed to be one of the five integral art forms in China, also known as Wushu. It was and still is compared to other arts and fields of study involving metaphysics such as Feng Shui, which is the study of land, and Bazi, the art of reading one's destiny.

The word Mien translates to face, and Xiang translates to the study of facial features. Ancient Taoist practitioners believed that a person's past is clearly apparent on their face, as it was recorded in the past. As such, you could easily tell a person's story by simply looking at their face. Many people confuse the art of Mien Shiang (which is all about face reading) with interpreting one's expressions; these two are completely different in practice. Mien Shiang can be conducted on expressionless faces as well. Facial features like the depth of one's eyes, the prominence of wrinkles and cheekbones, the length of the nose, and marks on the face, can all be read and analyzed to understand a person's history and even predict their future.

The Principles of Mien Shiang Include

· Three sections of the face – upper, middle, and lower

· Yin/Yang

· Five main organs of the face – eyes, ears, eyebrows, nose, and mouth

· Wrinkles, lines, moles, scars, and speckles

· The shape of the face

· Twelve Houses on a face

· Sheng Shiang – a person's sound or voice

· Nei Shiang – a person's chest, waist, shoulders, abdomen, neck, breasts, back, and forearms, among other body parts

· Gu Shiang – the practice of reading bones, including the skull

· Dong Shiang – a person's basic movement and behavioral pattern such as walking, crying, sleeping, eating, standing, and sitting.

Wu Xing is the art of studying the Five Elements, Five Phases, Five Agents, Five Processes, Five Planets, Five Stages, Five Virtues, Five Poisons, and Five Ways of different disciplines – from a person's innate energy to the medicinal properties of a plant. In essence, any subject can be studied by categorizing it into five stages of development.

With face reading, Wu Xing can be depicted as the Five Phases or Five Elements, namely wood, fire, metal, earth, and water. These elements are distinguished based on different facial features and represent a specific region of the face, but there is no specific designation; your face can be represented by one or more of these elements at a time.

The History of its Popularity and Skepticism

As time passed, the study of physiognomy evolved and began to be perceived as a scientific approach. By the 18th and 19th centuries, it was considered and used in forensics to identify criminals, but it was not of much use and partly discontinued thereafter. By the advent of the 20th century, physiognomy was discarded and has been relegated to the rank of a mere historical subject ever since.

That said, it was still used in various cultural works such as romantic novels, short stories, and literature dramas. Edgar Allan Poe's short stories and Oscar Wilde's *The Picture of Dorian Gray* briefly use physiognomy in their plots.

The face reading techniques that are followed and practiced today greatly differ from those employed a few centuries ago. The evolution and changes in ancient face reading techniques are also quite remarkable. You can still come across lengthy scriptures for effective face reading techniques in ancient Chinese classics and notice how these patterns of interpretations evolved.

In the 20th century, a French psychiatrist by the name of Louis Corman coined the term *morphopsychology*, which contends that the internal workings of people's bodies and other vital forces join to develop various face shapes. For instance, the expression of instinct is visible through round, full-bodied shapes, whereas self-preservation is expressed through flat or hollow shapes.

Several studies related to physiognomy have been conducted in modern times. Some research in the 1990s has established that honesty, warmth, and power were three personality traits that could be assessed using face reading. Another study on hockey players also revealed the correlation between a player's penalty minutes and their wide faces. Fast-forwarding to 2010, physiognomy was primarily considered as a part of machine learning to introduce facial recognition in artificial intelligence. Just by looking at a person's face, researchers could appraise their level of strength and prominent characteristics.

In 2017, yet another study shed light on an algorithm that could supposedly predict or detect a person's sexual orientation, which was eventually proven to be dangerous and false. Evidently, it was a topic of heated discussion and controversy.

Due to increased individuality and vulnerability in modern individuals, the practice of physiognomy is often considered discriminatory and insensitive, but this technique has been applied to understand human evolution and people's emotions in its authentic form. Because of these scientific and emotional implications, this pseudoscience is still practiced across the world, but with a more practical and prudent approach.

Physiognomy as it is Perceived Today

In today's world, plastic and cosmetic surgery have become quite popular. Many people might be asking themselves, "Will the face alterations caused by enhancement surgeries impact face reading in any way?" Cosmetic surgery is never the answer when you are unhappy with a certain face feature. To improve your exterior, you must work on the interior. For example, recurring facial acne and spots can be caused by a bad diet or an underlying health issue. By switching to more wholesome foods and treating the condition, you can get rid of these spots and discoloration, which will eventually give you a clear face. In parallel, you should learn to face and handle your insecurities. Working on your mental well-being and thought process is bound to bring subtle yet encouraging improvements in self-image. Other aspects that could alter your facial features could be experiences, behavior, tolerance, and your overall attitude.

As an art, the practice of face reading is relatively easier compared to techniques such as palm reading, since it is not as obvious and can be practiced without the person (or other people) noticing. In fact, whenever you meet someone, you might be reading their face instinctively, by unconscious reflex. You cannot figure out a person's character and intentions with just one meeting, which is where face reading can prove helpful. This is particularly beneficial in formal meetings or high-stress situations. For example, suppose you are meeting a potential business partner. There, you can determine whether they will be loyal, trustworthy, or capable of running a business and driving it to success.

Similarly, you can assess a person's character based on a date (birthdate) and ascertain whether they are fit to be your permanent partner. It applies in almost every setting.

A major issue, which was also prevalent in the past, is the way of living. Regardless of a person's nationality, culture, ethnicity, and social standing, everyone is expected to conform and live a certain pre-established way. The attributes a person is born with are conditioned by their elders, society, religion, and the media's expectations. Most of us are stuck in this loop, trying to live differently and detach ourselves from the environment we were born into. You either get a reward for behaving in an "acceptable" way or are punished and ostracized if you do not fit in. While certain behaviors are expected for the sake of morality and tradition, many individuals simply decide to change their outlook on life entirely.

As a result, most of us do not feel like "ourselves"; a part of us is missing. There comes a time in everyone's life when we feel lost and grow unkind towards our own selves. The expression of self-love gets lost along the way. Since your face is an open book to your soul, past, and destiny, you get to learn who you truly are and what you are destined to become. You get to know why you are this way and acquire the ability and power to change yourself for the better. At the same time, you also come to understand the people around you and why they show a certain behavior towards you. Ultimately, this helps you become the best version of yourself and empowers you with feelings of empathy and acceptance; you not only accept and love yourself but also let others be who they are and who they want to be. Down the line, you will no longer feel anger or hatred towards others, which will also help balance your mental health and grant you inner peace.

Chapter 2: Face Basics: The Facial Map

Now that you have acquired a solid background knowledge, this chapter is all about learning the basics of face reading and exploring the different sections of the face. With this practice knowledge, you can easily grasp a person's traits simply by looking at the shape of their face and studying their individual facial features.

Face Shapes

As established, your facial shape can indicate your character, prominent traits, and overall personality. Let's take a look at the basic face shapes and what they say about your personality.

Square Shape

For starters, square-faced individuals are usually driven and have good leadership qualities. They often dream about becoming CEOs or leading a company. If you meet a person with a square-shaped face and a broad forehead, it is likely that the person is dominant, unethical, and aggressive. Whenever you converse, they will be polite to you, but any form of crude or condescending comment can make them aggressive. They are also blessed with agile decision-making skills, which explains their leadership skills and entrepreneurial minds. They are highly driven and go to great lengths to make things happen, hence being stellar leaders. In parallel, they are also fit for the wrestling ring due to their combative behavior. A square-shaped face is often referred to as an "earth face" in traditional Chinese face reading.

Common Attributes of a Square Face

· **Pragmatism:** These people always have a practical approach to life. Whether it is in business, their studies, or their personal life, they will always take practical, thought-out decisions instead of considering their emotions. They often take a methodical approach in their work, which helps them excel in their endeavors.

· **Down to Earth:** They are grounded and humble and are hardly ever seen boasting about their achievements, wealth, or lifestyle.

· **Safe Players:** These people prefer to play it safe, as they fear taking risks. Whether it's their personal relationships or career, they would rather keep away from danger by sticking to conventions and norms.

· **Quiet and Reliable:** Should you give them any task, they will fulfill it and produce satisfying results, making them highly reliable. They are quiet, reserved, and would rather stay in their own zone.

· **Perceptive:** They have their own point of view, which they don't mind sharing. Others rely on their perceptive nature as they always seem to make logical, well-argued points.

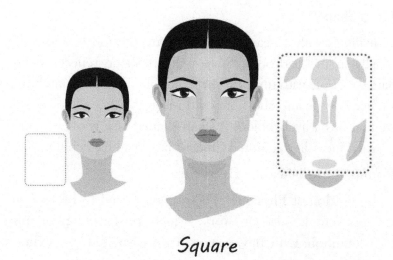

Square

Heart Shape

Individuals with a heart-shaped face are passionate and romantic, especially in the bedroom. Since a heart shape reflects feelings of romance, people with this face shape are often sexually uninhibited. If one's face is wide and short, it could mean that the person is sexually active and has a lively libido. A heart-shaped face is often referred to as a "wood face" in traditional Chinese face reading techniques.

Common Attributes of a Heart Face

· **Modest Physique:** These people tend to be lazy and do not enjoy outdoor work, which results in poor physical condition. Evidently, a sports career isn't the wisest choice for these individuals.

· **Responsible and Great Leaders:** These individuals are responsible and capable enough to lead a team to success.

· **Naturally Curious:** People with heart-shaped faces are naturally curious and always prepared to grow their knowledge and pick up new skills. They also spend most of their time analyzing new subjects and gathering knowledge from wherever they can.

· **Ability to See the Greater Picture**: They make effective decisions and are always closer to their goals thanks to their ability to step back and see the big picture. They are focused and pay attention to the smallest goals or milestones, which helps them reach the objectives rapidly.

· **High Mental Capacity:** People with a developed mental capacity are more likely to make intelligent decisions, which also makes them a proper fit as political figures and CEOs. They also have great persuasion skills.

A heart-shaped face also indicates that someone is a people pleaser and wants to be around others all the time. They are often considered ambiverts, standing halfway between introversion and extraversion, although that depends on the situation and circumstances. The way they define their relationships and leisure is a prominent trait in their personality. If you notice a woman with a recessed chin, slightly bigger nose and lips, and blunt jaws, it indicates that she is sociable and enjoys meeting new people. In contrast, women with a sharper jawline and a blunt or smaller nose are generally introverts and prefer to keep to themselves. They will not go out of their way to make new acquaintances unless absolutely necessary. Lastly, they are also great planners, which makes them proficient employees and managers.

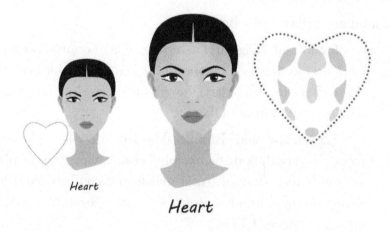

Heart

Heart

Round Shape

Oddly enough, a peculiar trait that this face shape relates to is snoring. Individuals with a round face tend to snore heavily, regardless of their age, weight, and overall state of health. While this is not true for all round-shaped individuals, the chances are highly likely. Also, the habit of uproarious snoring is not bound to just round-shaped faces but can also affect individuals with certain health issues. A round-shaped face is often referred to as a "water face" in traditional Chinese face reading techniques.

Common Attributes of a Round Face

· **Smart and Diligent:** These people are serious about their work due to their conscientiousness and self-established rules. Since they are also smart, they often succeed in carrying out the tasks put in front of them.

· **Diplomatic and Business-Minded:** People with round faces are very diplomatic, mainly because they want to play it safe and steer clear of trivial debates or conflicts. And their strong business minds encourage them to become successful entrepreneurs or CEOs.

· **Optimistic and Caring:** These people are highly optimistic and prefer to see positivity in negative situations. They prefer to learn from challenging circumstances and believe that everything happens for a reason. Everyone loves to be around them in light of their caring nature.

· **Creative and Intuitive:** These people are usually creative and have an exemplary imaginative power. As such, they are well-suited for creative jobs in art, content creation, or marketing. They have a strong intuition, which often saves them from sticky situations.

People with big eyes and arched or high eyebrows tend to agree with most things that are thrown at them. They usually have a narrow or short forehead. They agree with most people around them due to their openness and ability to accept different points of view without casting judgment. At times, these people also show complacency to others just to please them, even if they don't fundamentally agree. Lastly, they are dreamers and often have vivid sexual dreams.

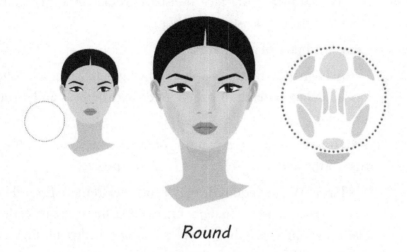

Round

Oval Shape

Oval shaped faces are the most attractive. People are instantly attracted to an oval face as it differs slightly from other common face shapes. In fact, people with oval faces are so good-looking that they are fit to partake in beauty pageants. An oval-shaped face is often referred to as a "metal face" in traditional Chinese face reading. It is characterized by perfect symmetry, chiseled jaws, and a sharp chin. Even if a person with an oval face doesn't have all these prominent features, they will show at least one of them.

Common Attributes of an Oval Face

· **A High IQ:** These people are highly intelligent and often win in debates thanks to their effective rhetoric and logical reasoning.

· **Honest:** They are always honest, which makes them trustworthy and loyal relative, friend, or spouse.

· **Firm:** When required, they can be extremely firm. They have a great sense of judgment, making them great leaders. Also, since they play by the rules and are forthright, they can be successful judges, diplomats, managers, or a similar role.

· **Self-Critical:** Oval-faced individuals can be somewhat hard on themselves. When things don't go according to their expectations, they regret their actions and criticize themselves, but they know how to learn from their mistakes and swiftly move forward.

· **Weak Physical Strength:** These individuals often lack physical strength, which is why they often fail in athletics. Those interested in a career in sports should rethink their decision.

Another prominent trait of people with this face shape is that they can widen their perspective and evaluate their future perspectives. They can see the bigger picture and decide accordingly. Also, these individuals are able to solve problems easily, which adds to their value as effective decision-makers. They keep track of their tasks expertly and work hard to fulfill them. A face shape that is equal in width and height is blessed with power and radiates a positive aura. Since they have the ability to look at the bigger picture, they can stay focused on achieving the milestones that will lead them to their ultimate objectives.

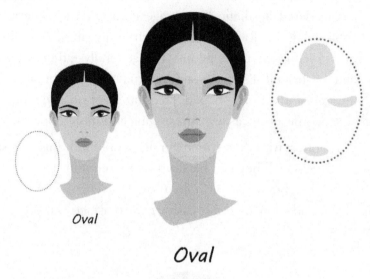

Oval

Oval

Diamond Shape

People with a diamond-shaped face are the most dependable and make friendly neighbors. If you need assistance, these are the people you can approach without any reservations. They tend to be more upright than others. A person with a diamond-shaped face often has a narrow jawline, high cheekbones, and a small chin. Even though this shape is considered aesthetically average compared to others, most people approach it due to its cheerful and friendly vibes. This also has to do with psychology; most people are generally either jealous or intimidated by beautiful people, as they may pose a threat to their social life. Since diamond-shaped faces are considered somewhat average, they come across as less threatening and more approachable.

In stark contrast with their friendly trait, people with this face shape may get angry easily. They can be short-tempered and quick to react. They are amiable, but if you push them over the edge, they are bound to strike back and show their aggressive nature, which can prove quite fierce.

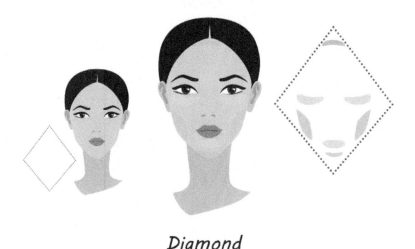

Diamond

Rectangular Shape

Much like square-shaped faces, people with this shape also make skilled leaders. Since a rectangular shape is often considered strong, it also reflects in the traits of those who bear this face shape. If you meet a person with a rectangle face, a broad forehead, high cheekbones, and sharp jaws, they are highly likely to have powerful leadership skills and be stronger than people with a narrow face. Rectangular-shaped faces are often compared to long faces. And while long faces have the same skillset and leadership qualities, the former makes for stronger and more effective leaders. You may notice that CEOs with rectangular faces tend to be more powerful and often drive their company towards commercial and financial success.

Like people with diamond-shaped faces, a major negative trait of those with rectangular faces is that they can be short-tempered and quickly aggressive. In extreme cases, these individuals may need anger management classes. On the plus side, they are great thinkers and often think with logic instead of emotions and instinct, but they are prone to overthinking and self-inflicted stress, which can ruin their decisions or plans.

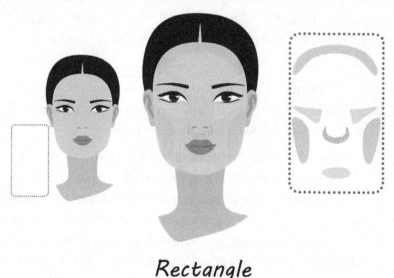

Rectangle

Triangle Shape

A triangle shape is also often referred to as a pearl-shaped face. It is characterized by a wide jawline and a narrow forehead. The chin is usually flared out and quite dominant compared to other facial features. People with this face shape often want to lead others and be in charge, which makes them superb business managers or company owners. If the forehead is too narrow, this reflects their unending urge to be in charge. They can go to any length to prove their leadership abilities and take control. Party planning and event managing are ideal career choices for them. Overall, this need to control and manage stems from their desire to succeed, which helps them reach their goals sooner and earn money through hard, honest work. A triangle-shaped face is often referred to as a "fire face" in traditional Chinese face reading.

Common Attributes of a Triangle Face

· **Bright and Illuminating:** These people spread joy and laughter around them, enhancing their capacity to attract others and build friendships. As soon as they enter any room, it lights up. This illuminating quality means they can convince people to agree with them and change their mindset with relative ease. It can be quite beneficial in certain settings, such as a PR or a sales job.

· **Forgiving:** They are too joyful and driven to hold grudges and believe that humans make mistakes. According to them, everyone should be given a second chance.

· **Sociable and Networking Skills:** Out in the working world, people with triangular faces make contacts easily, which is beneficial for their career and professional development. Since they can lead a team and are able to motivate others, they make excellent motivational speakers and presenters. They always seek an audience to showcase their skills and feel important.

· **Short Temper:** Triangle-shaped people get angry easily. Although they are highly driven and talented, their short temperament can get in the way and spoil valuable opportunities. In intense situations, these people may get distracted from their goals and see their success delayed due to their quick and vehement temper.

Individuals with a triangular face shape are highly extroverted can make friends without pretense. They are fun to be around and exude happiness and positive vibes. They shine brightly and want others to shine as well, which explains their inspiring and motivating nature.

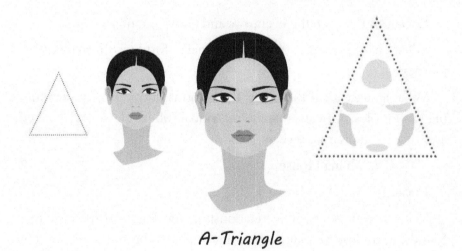

A-Triangle

Understanding the Twelve Houses – One of the Prominent Jargons of Mien Shiang

Also known as the Twelve Palaces or Twelve Sections, the Twelve Houses refer to the twelve basic ways of reading faces. The number twelve is significant in face reading because ancient Chinese physiognomy books established twelve sections of the human face. The location of these twelve houses aligns with the individual's fortune. In parallel, other factors believed to influence the face pertain to these twelve houses' arrangement, shape, gloss, and color.

1. Life House

Location: Between the eyebrows and above the nose.

What it represents: The individual's fortune throughout his journey.

What it suggests: If the line is thick and is devoid of any fine lines, pits, and moles, it means that the individual will be blessed with wealth and success in their later years.

2. Sibling House

Location: At the eyebrows

What it represents: The relationship one has with their siblings, friends, and close acquaintances. The right eyebrow stands for their relationship with their sisters, and the left eyebrow suggests their relationship with their brothers.

What it suggests: If the individual has thick and smooth eyebrows, they have an extended circle of trustworthy friends. On the other hand, if someone has messy eyebrows, it means that their friends are vile.

3. Wealth House

Location: At the apex and wings of the nose.

What it represents: How a person will perform in their professional career and how much wealth they will amass.

What it suggests: If the wings and apex of one's nose are bright and full, it could indicate good opportunities coming their way. In contrast, a person who has an apex with a mole might struggle in their career and lack opportunities for a prolonged period, but if the apex appears bloodshot or harbors pimples, it could indicate unexpected financial losses.

4. Health House

Location: Bridge of the nose.

What it represents: An individual's state of health and the quality of their physical attributes.

What it suggests: If the bridge of the nose is glossy and without any scars, breakage, lines, pit, or mole, it indicates fortunate health and happiness.

5. Marriage House

Location: Corner of the eye.

What it represents: The health of a relationship or a marriage.

What it suggests: If the corner of your eye is glossy and full, it indicates a healthy relationship and a long marriage. If it is sinking or has moles, it could predict a tortuous relationship. While a dark left corner for a woman means that her spouse is having an affair or is partaking in extra-marital indulgences, her dark right usually means that she is facing obstacles in her marriage.

6. Children's House

Location: Below the eyes.

What it represents: The health, occurrences, and information related to your children.

What it suggests: If your eyes have bags under them or if the skin is sinking, this may indicate that you have no children. If the area and skin under your eyes are plump, it indicates that you will be or are already blessed with kids. But it shouldn't be overly plump as it could predict unfavorable outcomes. If the under-eye area is filled with wrinkles or has moles, it means that you worry too much about your children's well-being and future. In men, the left of the Children's House indicates sons, whereas the right side suggests daughters.

7. Career House

Location: Middle of the forehead.

What it represents: Your position in your workplace and career.

What it suggests: If the Career House is slightly raised and goes up to your nose, it indicates that you will perform well at work and excel in your career, but if it has wrinkles, pits, lines, or moles, it could mean potential issues with your professional life, such as getting fired, job loss, or prolonged unemployment. Chiang Kai-shek, a renowned Chinese historical political figure, has the desired Career House.

8. Traveling House

Location: At the sideburns.

What it represents: Your travel journey, opportunities, and travel fortune.

What it suggests: If your sideburns have wrinkles, pits, lines, or moles, it means that there could be potential issues with your upcoming travel plans. So, it is advised to stay at home and avoid unnecessary travel. On the other hand, if they are glossy and plump, you are safe to travel and await enriching trips in the future.

9. Assistant House

Location: On each side of the chin.

What it represents: The amount of help you get from your subordinates, spouse, or assistants, and how competent they are.

What it suggests: If the sides of your chin are straight and smooth, it indicates that your subordinates are helpful and will guide you throughout the journey. But if they are sunken, it could mean that your aids are not competent enough to help you in your work. It could also mean that they are dishonest and that you should not entirely trust them.

10. Parents House

Location: Above the starting point of the eyebrow.

What it represents: Your parents. The right eyebrow point represents your mother, and the left eyebrow point represents your father.

What it suggests: If the starting point of your eyebrows is glossy, plump, and smooth, it indicates the longevity and health of your parents. But if it is brazen, rough, or has a mole or a pit, it could considerably affect these two aspects. In this case, make sure that you keep good track of your parents' health.

11. Property House

Location: At the upper eyelid.

What it represents: A person's property, inheritance, residence, dwelling, and family love.

What it suggests: The Property House is apparent when the upper eyelid is raised, particularly the spot furthest away from the eyebrow. In this case, the child finds it easier to inherit ancestral property, and it is often given to them without asking. However, if the eyebrow is too close to the upper eyelid, or if you notice that someone has a sunken eye socket, it typically means that they will face an issue in inheriting their ancestral property.

12. Fortune and Emotion House

Location: Above the eyebrow bend and at the sides of the Career House.

What it represents: Fortune, emotional health, and mental health.

What it suggests: If the Fortune and Emotion House is plump, it means that you are optimistic and at peace with yourself. But if it is sunken, it could indicate a negative mindset and pessimistic nature. It could also mean that you lack self-confidence. Finally, if the Fortune and Emotion House is a dark color, the person might suffer soon due to their bad luck.

Heaven, Human, and Earth

Ancient Chinese face reading also followed another method for reading faces and marking their attributes, namely with the sections of Heaven, Human, and Earth. The area spanning from the forehead to the point of the upper eyebrows is known as Heaven, the middle part between the upper eyebrows and the tip of the nose is called Human, and the last section of the face, below the nose down to the chin, is called Earth. Heaven is associated with one's early years or youth. Human is associated with an individual's middle years, and Earth is associated with their old age. If you notice any scars, discoloration, or scabs in any particular section, it can relate to issues in the person's life during that relevant period. For example, if you witness discoloration near a person's chin area, it means that the person may suffer in their old age.

If the marks are temporary, this indicates that the person will suffer temporarily and overcome the hardship once the difficult phase is over. So, before you read a person's face through their mark, ask whether the spot is a temporary bruise or a permanent birthmark. Even if there is a speck of light on someone's face, it could still mean something. Generally, any form of discoloration or divination relates to the intuition of the face reader.

According to the ancient Chinese face reading tradition, these three areas depict the following attributes:

1. Heaven

This section is located between the hairline and the tip of the upper eyebrow, representing a person's childhood and their fate during their early years.

Positive aspects: If the area is free of spots, marks, bumps, scars, discoloration, or any other apparent flaw, it means that the person has had a happy childhood and a good start in life. It denotes a healthy relationship with their parents, friends, and peers. Also, the person was blessed with remarkable education, values, and a healthy lifestyle.

Negative aspects: On the contrary, if the person shows scars, bumps, lines, or discoloration within the Heaven section, it could mean that they have had a troubled or traumatic childhood, which could also affect their later life stages. While a wide forehead is generally preferable, it is not entirely desirable for women as it could foretell poor relationships. If the disfigurement is noted on the right side, it is harmful to women. In contrast, a left-side disfigurement is undesirable for men. Most people have lines on their forehead, which suggests a person's major traits, while some lines indicate luck; others stand for hardships and misfortune.

2. Human

The middle section of a person's face indicates their traits and fate during adulthood.

Positive aspects: If the area is free of spots, marks, bumps, scars, discoloration, or any other apparent flaw, it means that the person will be productive, happy, and is promised a great career. They will be blessed with a desirable professional life and excel to reach success. It also means that they will enjoy happy and stable relationships.

Negative aspects: On the contrary, if the person has scars, bumps, lines, or discoloration within the Human section, it could mean that they might face a blockage in their love life and career. They can see their success delayed or even lose their jobs. Their relationship could be affected due to an unexpected breakup or failed marriage. Besides the scars and coloration, the Human section's length and size also matter; if it is longer than the other two sections, it means that the person is determined and driven to fulfill their goals. It also portrays a self-disciplined personality and character.

3. Earth

The bottom section of the face, traditionally referred to as the Earth section, spans from the bottom of the nose to the chin's end.

Positive aspects: If the area is free of spots, marks, bumps, scars, discoloration, or any other apparent flaw, it means that the person will have a fulfilling old age with stable, long-term relationships and loving kids. It also indicates a successful career and a comfortable retirement life. At the same time, it could also mean that they are blessed with good health despite advanced age.

Negative aspects: On the contrary, if the person has scars, bumps, lines, or discoloration within the Earth section, it could mean that they might have an unhappy old age. They might either suffer from poor health or undergo unexpected loss, leaving them lonely in their later years.

This method of reading a face is the easiest and most accessible and can predict a person's life throughout different stages. If you quickly want to read someone and warn them of any possible negative occurring, this may help them take the necessary actions and turn the situation around. If any among these three divisions seems more compressed than others, it signifies that the person has had or will endure a challenging life during that period. For example, if their forehead (Heaven section) is smaller than the Human or Earth section, they experienced a difficult childhood.

Thirteen Divisions

Another detailed way of reading someone's face in traditional Chinese philosophy is by dividing the face into thirteen sub-sections, starting from the bottom of the hairline to the chin's lower tip. Unlike the Twelve Houses explained above, these thirteen divisions are more specific in terms of location and alignment. The divisions begin from the top of the forehead and stretch down to the chin, spreading across horizontally over the length of one's face.

The three main sections (Heaven, Human, and Earth) are further divided into 13 sections. Here is a detailed breakdown of each:

1. Tien Chung

Location: Directly below the hairline, the first point - in the Heaven section.

What it suggests: Since it is located in the Heaven section, it represents a person's life during childhood. If it is free of scabs, discoloration, or any other marks, it indicates that the person has had or will have a happy and healthy childhood. At the same time, they will enjoy fulfilling relationships with their parents, teachers, friends, and acquaintances, not only in their childhood but also in a similarly joyous experience throughout their youth. But if there are any marks or spots in that specific area, it could indicate a painful childhood full of hardship and suffering. If you notice dark marks or veins in that area, it could mean that the person might have suffered from a serious accident. You should also warn the person of a sudden loss, which could be either financial or pertain to a personal relationship. If it's a widow's peak, this could signify that their father might pass away before their mother.

2. Tien Ting

Location: Below Tien Chung, in the middle of the forehead – in the Heaven section.

What it suggests: This mostly relates to family relationships, particularly with the mother and father. If the spot is marked or colored, it could point to negative circumstances in their personal relationships. Also, a mark in this spot indicates dishonesty and instantly reveals that a person is not speaking the truth.

3. Ssu K'ung

Location: Just above the center of the eyebrows – in the Heaven section.

What it suggests: It represents an individual's fortune and career. No discoloration or an even complexion means that the person shouldn't worry about their career. They are bound to succeed professionally. If you notice any discoloration or spot at this point, it could indicate an obstacle in the individual's career. It might be temporary or permanent, depending on the person's situation and history of discoloration (resulting from an accident or acne scars).

4. Chung Cheng

Location: Around the center of the eyebrows – in the Heaven section.

What it suggests: If this area harbors a mark, spot, or any form of discoloration, it indicates bad luck. The person is either indecisive or unable to work hard to achieve their goals. It can also imply a person's inability to enhance their personal image, which can hinder their life plans and future goals. If the spot is dented, this may be the sign of below-average intellect and poor assessment skills. Lastly, any spot, mark, or bump means an uneventful social life and the inability to make new friends; the person will hardly have any friends or meet any in the future. But if the spot is clear and smooth, it indicates that they will make wise decisions, act on their plans, work hard to achieve their goals, and have a gratifying social life.

5. Yin T'ang

Location: Right above the center of the eyebrows – in the Heaven section.

What it suggests: If the eyebrows meet, either fully or partly, this also indicates bad luck and could mean that the person does not receive enough respect. In Chinese face reading, this is believed to be one of the most visible and obvious forms of bad fortune. Any spot, mole, bump, or discoloration in this area reveals bad luck in terms of inheritance, health, or adoption. It is also considered a sign of future imprisonment. If the individual is over forty and shows wrinkles or lines in this area, they have nothing much to worry about, except a bit of stress or tension that could affect their health. Someone below the age of forty with these wrinkles or creases is usually stressed about their career, personal relationships, and other important aspects of their life. They also have a jealous nature and may be easily intimidated by others. Flaws in this area also indicate the possibility of having faced difficulties during the youth, but if the spot is smooth, clear, and healthy, it means that the person will perform well in business and is likely to gain an inheritance.

6. Shan Gen

Location: The center of the eyebrows or at the Third Eye – in the Human section.

What it suggests: As mentioned above, a unibrow primarily suggests bad luck. If the spot is gray or shows dark discoloration, it can mean that the person may be suffering from an illness. If you see a green patch in this area, this can reveal adulterous practices. Any other form of spot, mole, or bump indicates digestive and stomach related issues or even imprisonment. It can also mean that the person is looking forward to emigration. If the spot is clear, though, it means that they are blessed with good health and stability in their life.

7. Men Shang

Location: Below the central point of the eyebrows, the starting point of the nose – in the Human section.

What it suggests: A clear spot indicates good health and stable personal relationships, especially at a young age. If the spot is dark, the child can fall ill or face sudden health complications. If the spot has discoloration or moles, it indicates digestive and stomach- related issues for both them and their partner. If not this, then the individual might also face trouble in their personal relationship, specifically with their spouse.

8. Shou Shang

Location: At the center of the nose bridge – in the Human section.

What it suggests: If a female has a mole or discoloration on the bridge of their nose, it could indicate issues in their personal or romantic relationship. They should also warn their husband of sudden illness or health issues. The woman may face many hardships in her life, especially concerning relationships and long-term involvement. Men with similar discoloration or moles in this area may also face health problems, even if they are not yet married. If a person's nasal bone structure appears bumpy or somehow out of shape, it could cause issues in their business or career. But a smooth nose bridge void of any spot or discoloration signifies success in their profession, better health, and steady personal relationships.

9. Chun Tou

Location: Tip of the nose – in the Human section.

What it suggests: If the tip of one's nose has moles, spots, or discoloration, it indicates bad luck in all aspects of their life – personal life, relationships, career, health, and the like. However, if the tip is free of blackheads, marks, spots, moles, or otherwise, it points to good luck and happy fortune in all areas of their life.

10. Jen Chung

Location: At the recessed spot above the lips and just below the nose – in the Earth section.

What it suggests: This recessed area, which is also known as the philtrum of the fallen line, also represents a person's luck. Unlike other spots that only denote luck through color and texture, this spot tells a person's story through its shape and depth. If the philtrum is wide at the base and narrow on top, it signifies that the person will be blessed with riches and healthy children. In this case, the dent between the top and bottom of the grooved area should be neither too flat nor too deep. Along with wealth and kids, they will also achieve respect and a higher social status. If the philtrum is wider on top and narrow at the bottom, this can signify difficulties in having kids. In men, this shape indicates a sour nature and dubious ethics. The person may face issues with others and often get involved in fights due to a lack of proper manners. Lastly, they will also face complications in their personal relationships.

If the grooved part has a middle line in the center that goes down, it means that the person will have children later in life. But if the grooved area is bent ever so slightly, it means that the individual will suffer in their social life because of their deceitful nature. They may experience a lack of respect and recognition and find themselves subjected to unpopularity. They also run the risk of not being able to have any children.

11. Shui Hsing

Location: At the mouth, over the lips – in the Earth section.

What it suggests: If the corners of the mouth face downwards, this could mean poor health and strenuous relationships. If the lips are dull and lack color, it is a typical sign of bad fortune. Conversely, full pink lips indicate prosperity and good luck. The corner of one's mouth, if turned upwards, denotes happiness, good luck, and healthy marriage. Even if the lips are temporarily discolored, this can reveal intermittent issues in one's relationship or health.

12. Ch'eng Chiang

Location: At the recess below the lips and above the chin – in the Earth section.

It is suggested that men who lack hair in this small gap may suffer from poor digestive health and stomach issues. This is also the case with women who harbor spots, marks, or discoloration in this area. Their stomachs are often weak, and they must closely monitor their food intake and follow a strict diet. If the gap seems temporarily discolored, especially during a specific time of the day, like mornings, it can mean that the person may face issues during their travels. These individuals are advised to avoid water or boat travel, especially during the day (if the discoloration is noted in the morning, for example).

13. Ti ko

Location: Tip of the chin – in the Earth section.

What it suggests: The last section of the face, which is also at the bottom of the center line and known as Ti ko, indicates appearance and emotions. If the chin is round and smooth, the person may have a strong personality and appearance. If they have a pointed chin, especially sideways, it means that the person is unapologetic and holds grudges against others. A sharp chin is also undesirable as it indicates bad fortune. If this area shows moles, scars, or any form of discoloration, it can be a foretelling sign of sickness, major financial losses, accidents, or an issue with inheritance. But if the chin is free of discoloration, moles, and scars, it indicates good luck, stability, and a successful and rewarding career.

These thirteen points appear from the top to the bottom of the face, as illustrated. They can be easily remembered thanks to the three divisions of the face – Heaven, Human, and Earth.

Chapter 3: The Five Elements and Personalities

This section covers the five traditional elements of wood, fire, earth, metal, and water, which coincide with seasons or any individual's personality traits. This is the Taoist Mien Shiang theory. Before we learn about these five elements and their meanings, let's first understand why such an analysis is relevant. Since the five elements and the season associated with each are a natural part of our universe and ecosystem, they relate to our natures. Basically, all of us are our own system, making the parallel with nature easier, but since we all have different fortunes and upbringing, our characteristics and personalities vary. So, this justifies the relationship between ourselves and the forces of nature.

Simultaneously, the inclusion of these natural elements with seasons encompasses all kinds of individuals, giving everyone a chance with expanded horizons and a combination of different traits. Depending on the elements and particular combination, they can be both an introvert and extrovert in different situations. This correlation explains our dominant traits, weaknesses, and personalities that could be quite impactful. For instance, an individual can relate to spring while having traits of winter.

By learning about these elements and applying them to the study and practice of face reading, you will better understand a person's behavior and personal life. At times, we are too quick to judge someone based on their demeanor and outer appearance; not many comprehend that they might be going through a difficult time or have suffered a loss, causing their bitter behavior. Once you learn to read a person's traits, you will be able to relate to their predicament on a deeper level and understand them better. You will gain answers to questions such as:

· Why did they behave the way they did?

· Were they under stress? If so, what is the cause?

· Why do they feel they can go through life without a plan?

· Why do they always stay alone? Why do they rarely go out?

· How do they deal with their relatives and friends?

· How are they so open? How come they never feel shy?

· Why do they never fully express themselves?

· Why are they always angry or frustrated?

In what follows, we will learn more about these elements, seasons, and the relationship between them, in an attempt to understand and interpret a person's unique personality traits.

The 5 Elements and What they Mean

1. Wood

Association with the season: Spring and the energy of this season.

What it signifies: The spring season epitomizes rebirth, growth, and rejuvenation. Just like flowers and trees grow in the presence of sunlight, this element signifies moving forward towards the light. It is also about snapping out of stagnation and dullness. The Wood element in a person indicates movement, evolution, and growth. If you block the path of a person who represents the Wood element, it could delay their progress due to the inability to move forward and find balance.

Association with facial features: The person with this element has a well-defined eyebrow shape and a strong jaw. The shape of their face is generally either rectangular or square.

2. Fire

Association with the season: Summer and the peak of this season.

What it signifies: Summer represents vibrancy, growth, light, and joy. Just like bees roam around in search of nectar, flowers bloom, and the air gets fresher, an individual with this element will be happy, vibrant, and always searching for ways to achieve their goals. More often than not, the person with the Fire element will have an attractive and positive personality. They will be naturally curious and try to pick up new skills whenever and wherever they can.

Association with facial features: The person may have freckles and dimples on their cheeks and chin. Their facial features are usually pointed, and their eyes are wide. You may notice a sparkle in their eyes. Whenever they speak, their eyes grow wide open and shimmer. Their smile adds to their positive aura and brightens up their surroundings.

3. Earth

Association with the season: Late summer and the harvest in this season.

What it signifies: In the same way people come together to collect the season's harvest, this element represents a person's sense of unity. It also indicates abundance in one's life. If a person with the Earth element is not blessed with abundance, they will seek comfort and attention from their friends and family, encouraging them to make new friends and contacts as well. They also swear by comfort, especially in their home.

Association with facial features: The features of this person are usually plump and round. Typically, a person with this element will have full lips, large eyes, plump cheeks, and a round face.

4. Metal

Association with the season: Autumn/Fall.

What it signifies: Just like in fall, when people realize the importance of sunlight, greenery, and freshness, those with the Metal element will want to keep things and hold on to them tightly. It is difficult for them to let things and people go. Whether it's a fun outing with their friends or a tasty meal, they will savor every moment and extract as much joy from it as possible. Whenever you want to relinquish memories of any experience, you should always turn to an individual who possesses this element. At the same time, it is easy for them to let go of things, too; if you hurt them or if they feel that something is no longer precious, they will never think twice before letting it go. Just like trees let go of their dead leaves, individuals with the Metal element also shed anew.

Association with facial features: The face of this person is generally symmetrical and spaced out. Their features are sharp and pointed. A person with this element may have clear skin, high arched eyebrows, sharp cheekbones, and a pointed nose.

5. Water

Association with the season: Winter.

What it signifies: Both water and winter represent depth and darkness. Just like a sea or ocean is deep and mysterious, individuals with this sign also portray a mysterious personality and often prefer to be left alone. They can appear one way on the surface but be different and secretive underneath. Even if they are left alone or in darkness for a while, they don't seem to mind. In accordance with the proverb, "Silent water runs deep," they have a lot going on inside their minds but hardly ever express or reveal anything.

Association with facial features: The chin of this person may be quite prominent. They may also have large ears, a rounded forehead, and bags or puffiness under their eyes that give them a tired and solemn look.

How to Read the Elements (What Each Facial Feature Suggests)

Now, apart from these basic elements and the shape of one's face, individual features also denote hidden meanings and traits in a person.

Let's take a closer look at what these features reveal:

Eyebrows

Your eyebrows represent your luck and the state of your relationship with your siblings. They also speak of a person's social life and their ability to make connections. A unibrow suggests that someone can be easily triggered and willing to get into a fight or an argument over petty issues. This is also the case with eyebrows that barely meet. Ideally, a pair of eyebrows that represent good luck is often well-groomed, longer than the length of the eyes, and draws a slight curve.

In addition, the direction of your eyebrows can also point to various meanings.

> · If the eyebrows point downwards (arched at the starting point and slanting towards the end), it means that the person is kind, generous, and always straightforward. They are also open-minded.

> · If the eyebrows point upwards (arched at the starting point and towards the end), it means that the person is highly ambitious and motivated to achieve their goals. They like to be competitive and will work hard to win. This explains why they despise losing.

· If the eyebrows are too close to the eyes, it means that the person is an introvert who prefers to keep to themselves. They are usually shy, conservative, and cannot talk to people with confidence and ease.

Common Traits Based on the Shape of Your Eyebrows

· **Curved Eyebrows:** These people tend to build connections with others easily and make the environment more comfortable for everyone around them. Since they are people-oriented, they make an effort to connect with others by first understanding them. If you want to explain a concept to these people, use practical examples to make it simpler and keep them engaged.

· **Angled Eyebrows:** People with angled eyebrows have leadership qualities and want to lead a team in every situation. Whether it's a casual party or a business presentation, they always like to stay in command. Now, when it comes to being right and making a decision, their stubborn nature never fails to show up. They work hard to prove that they are right. And while they may very well be, the effort to prove it can come across as pretentious and off-putting. Lastly, they are focused and headstrong in whatever they set their minds to.

· **Straight Eyebrows:** These people are logical, practical, and driven by information that relies on analysis and proof. If you want these people to concede a point or agree with you, the best bet is to present them with factual and verifiable data. They will never let their emotions take over, instead of resorting to logic and practicality to make a decision or evaluate a situation.

Eyes

Big bright eyes are attractive and tend to diminish instances of social awkwardness, which is a dominant trait of people with conjoined eyebrows. If the white part of the eye is clear, it means that they can easily make friends. Often, these people are the most popular in their vast social circles. As the saying goes, one's eyes are the windows to their soul, which has never rung truer with these individuals.

Besides this, the direction of your eyeballs and the under-eye area also suggests various meanings.

> · If the eyeball is closer to the bottom eyelid, the white part is visible on the top and both sides of the eyes. This is known as "Upper Three White-eyes" and indicates that the person is unfaithful, selfish, and does not obey the law. This is why they are also known as Snake eyes.

· If the eyeball is closer to the upper eyelid, the white part is visible on the bottom and both sides of the eyes. This is called "Under Three White-eyes" and indicates the person is self-centered, generous to their friends, stubborn, and prefers to take the lead in all kinds of settings.

· Also known as the Children's Palace, the under-eye area indicates a person's luck in having kids. The under-eye area, if full, indicates that the person will be lucky enough to have kids with great health.

· If the under-eye area is sunken, dark, discolored, or bears any scar, it means that the person may struggle to have children. If they do, their offspring may face health complications during or after birth.

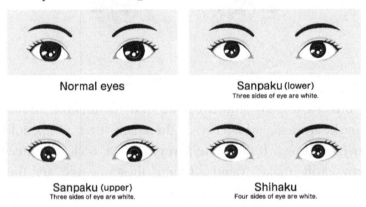

Normal eyes

Sanpaku (lower)
Three sides of eye are white.

Sanpaku (upper)
Three sides of eye are white.

Shihaku
Four sides of eye are white.

Traits Based on the Size and Color of Your Eyes

· **Small Eyes:** These people are usually narrow-minded and focus on a methodical, pragmatic approach when undertaking projects. They are highly selective and get deep into the subjects that grab their attention. Basically, it's all or nothing for them. They are also meticulously organized in their work.

· **Big Eyes:** These people are curious and open-minded. Their intellect aligns with their curiosity to produce things that are completely outside of the box. While they have strong imaginative power, they can get distracted easily. Their creativity is praiseworthy, and their hypersensitive nature is often misunderstood.

· **Black Eyes:** These people are highly mysterious and quiet but have a lot going inside beyond their stark facade. Some people may even have psychic powers. They want to know more about those around them, yet rarely open up or share details about them.

· **Brown Eyes:** Brown-eyed people are blessed with all Earth qualities, which include creativity, fertility, courage, energy, and endurance. They favor experiences and adventures over material possessions. Also, they want to be in and around nature as much as possible. They prefer to be independent but can easily collaborate with others when the circumstances call for it.

· **Hazel Eyes:** These eyes are not just beautiful to admire but also give the carrier something to showcase their carefree and courageous nature. They are always looking for someone who knows how to express their feelings. These people can be highly sensitive, too.

· **Green Eyes:** Green is the color of nature and Earth. A person with green eyes is more nature-oriented and is typically attracted to what's fresh and organic. They believe in healthy eating and living, as well as in spiritual energy and mystical studies. They also tend to be very compassionate and generous.

· **Blue Eyes:** Blue eyes are not just attractive; they portray a high sense of self-awareness. People with blue eyes are very curious and observant of their surroundings. This is because they cannot rely on other people and hardly trust anyone in a heartbeat, but they are still warm and kind towards others.

· **Gray Eyes:** Individuals with gray eyes have admirable internal strength. They are emotionally robust and invulnerable, but their wisdom and heterodox views make them somehow moody and irritable, especially when someone does not agree with their beliefs or viewpoints.

Forehead

The forehead typically represents a person's power in formal settings, such as a large company. If the forehead is broad or high, it means that the person possesses strong power and is the head of any entity. If it is low, it can indicate a lack of effective and inspiring leadership.

Additionally, a Broad or a High Forehead Also Denotes the Following Traits in a Person:

Confidence: These people are highly confident and seem to own the room as soon as they step foot in it. As a result, they attract others towards them and can reap many beneficial opportunities along the way.

Maturity: You will hardly find these people getting into childish banter, as they prefer to handle delicate matters the way grown-ups do. If you need any help to make wise decisions, these people are your go-to.

Practical and Good Financial Management Skills: This is why they make great accountants. Also, they never weigh in their emotions to make decisions. They always choose a more practical approach, especially on the job.

Early Success: Thanks to their pragmatism, confidence, maturity, and inherent leadership skills, these people always succeed earlier than their peers. They are go-getters and do not stop until their final goal is fulfilled.

The Size or Type of One's Forehead Declares:

High Forehead: These people are curious, ready to learn, and excel at complex subjects like mathematics and physics. Also, they always want to be sure of their decisions and of what their choices entail, as they are not particularly keen on taking risks and prefer to play it safe. They are highly secretive and can keep secrets as well. They will encourage you to take methodical steps yourself to achieve your goals with flying colors.

Average Forehead: Similarly, these individuals are highly intelligent and curious. They inspire others around them to work hard, think positively, and keep their focus. Their intuitive nature and problem-solving ability make them invaluable company assets, which helps them perform well in their career.

Low Forehead: These people hate being caged and would rather stay free. Also, their spontaneous nature enables them to make quick and decisive choices. They do not think before acting and make spontaneous decisions, which may push them towards failure. Nevertheless, they have a great sense of judgment that often brings about favorable outcomes.

FOREHEAD SHAPES IN PROFILE

Straight	Slopped	Convex	Wavy

FOREHEAD SHAPES IN FULL FACE

Tall and Wide	Tall and Narrow	Low and Wide

So, by reading a person's forehead and analyzing its shape and size, you can determine their level of intelligence, expertise, and how well they perform professionally.

Ears

A person's ears signify their childhood, usually between one and fourteen years of age. The ears also represent a person's ancestral luck.

Low ears, which are farther away from the head, are generally a sign of low intellect. High ears that are also closer to the head means that the person is highly intelligent. They not only excel in their studies and work but also as leaders.

The Thickness of the Ears Also Suggests Various Meanings

· Thick ears close to the head indicate a person's sensitive nature, thoughtfulness, and the ability to organize and plan (desks, meetings, or any other professional endeavor).

· If the ears are thick and high (imagine the handle of a teapot), it means that the person will gain success at a young age thanks to their intellectual capabilities. In parallel, they will also enjoy the fame that comes with these hard-earned achievements.

· A person's earlobes also suggest certain strong traits about them. If they are thick and full, it means that they were raised in a happy, healthy, and wealthy family. They have had constant support from their family from the beginning and still do.

DIFFERENT HUMAN EAR SHAPES

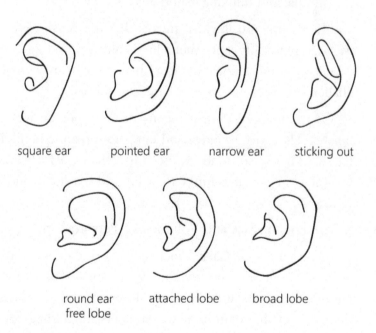

square ear   pointed ear   narrow ear   sticking out

round ear   attached lobe   broad lobe
free lobe

Mouth and Lips

Also representing the water element, a person's mouth usually does the talking, which is an effective way to make quick judgments. A lopsided and crooked mouth is a sign of poor communication skills. This, in turn, means that the person is not confident enough and lacks the ability to make friends. If a person has a large mouth, it often means that they are generous and kind.

The Shape and Position of the Lips Also Suggest Various Meanings

· If the ends of one's lips point downwards, it means that the person is shy, conservative, suspicious, and unhappy most of the time. They are not particularly friendly and drive people away because of their cold, stubborn demeanor.

· If the ends of one's lips point upwards, it means that the person is confident, positive, cheerful, and friendly. They attract people towards them and befriending them is always a pleasurable and fulfilling experience.

· If the lips are thick, it means that the person is kind as well as physically and mentally healthy, but they are not especially good at speaking in public, which can be a serious challenge in their professional and social lives.

· If the lips are thin, it means that the person is a gossip fanatic. They love to judge and talk about people behind their backs. They also tend to be very chatty, which may be favorable in social settings to avert awkwardness and build rapport.

Traits Based on the Size and Volume of a Person's Lips

· **Thick or Full Lips:** Thick lips are rather attractive and add to a person's beauty. These people tend to be very confident, warm, and always look forward to learning new things. They thrive on honing their skills and adding new ones to their set. They also appreciate those who give back and care about sharing new experiences with others. Finally, they like to meet new people and make friends.

· **Thin Lips:** These people prefer quality over quantity and are usually extremely picky. This is because they are attracted to the finer things. They prefer objects, thoughts, or food that is presented well; in other words, presentation matters greatly to them. They are sophisticated and want to do things their way. That said, they do not stop others from doing things the way they see fit.

LIP SHAPES

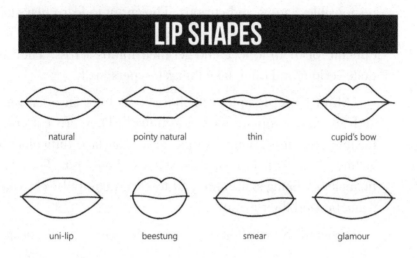

| natural | pointy natural | thin | cupid's bow |

| uni-lip | beestung | smear | glamour |

Nose

The shape of your nose measures your wealth. People with large noses are usually wealthier than those with thin and snubbed noses. And while beauty standards favor small, well-defined noses, people with naturally thicker noses are luckier as far as wealth and overall life success.

The Shape and Bridge of Your Nose Also Suggests Various Meanings

· If the nose bridge is tall and has thick wings at the base, it means that the person is strong-willed, sincere, popular in their social circle, and has the ability to grow rich and successful. This is also known as the Garlic Nose.

· If the nose wings are thick and full, it indicates that the person will be blessed with money. It will not be difficult for them to gather a great amount of wealth, either with luck, through hard work, or both.

Traits Based on the Size and Shape of a Person's Nose

· **Long Nose:** People with long noses are highly responsible, caring, and curious. They want to learn new skills and show a sense of practicality in their approaches, but it is difficult for them to love and get their minds across. They are quite serious and often take things too personally.

· **Short Nose:** People with short noses have an open mind and are always up for new adventures. They are extremely flexible and dependable. While they may face difficulties in getting along with others, they still try their best. They lack financial planning skills and tend to spend compulsively, often living beyond their means.

· **Pointed Nose:** Pointed noses are somehow associated with femininity. These people's strong intuitive power is remarkable. They are often drawn to culture and arts, especially music.

· **Flat Nose:** People with flat noses are loyal, patient, and hard-working. They will do anything to succeed and put in maximum effort to reach their personal and professional goals.

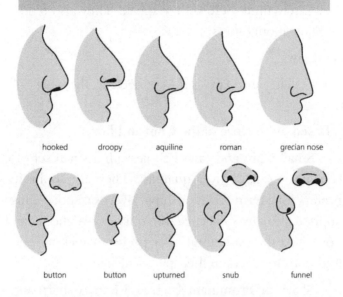

hooked   droopy   aquiline   roman   grecian nose

button   button   upturned   snub   funnel

Tongue

The tongue as a facial feature is rarely considered in face reading, as it is not always obvious or immediately perceived (unless, of course, you ask the other person to stick their tongue out for a reading, which we do not recommend). Since the tongue is a crucial part of face reading in several studies, learning about it can be greatly beneficial and complement your knowledge.

The Shape and Length of the Tongue Denotes Various Meanings

· If the tongue is short, it means that the person lacks discipline and personal drive. They can hardly focus on their roles and are hardly ever competitive. They also tend to lack ambition.

· If the tongue is long and thick, it shows that the person is able to learn new languages with ease. They are also quite proficient in communication and self-expression.

· If the tongue is long and thin, it means that the person is very talkative and can make others uncomfortable, seeing as they rarely think before they speak. They also tend to babble and talk about others.

Chin and Jaws

Since the chin and jaws are connected, they are often read together.

Traits Based on the Size of the Chin and Jaw

· **Small Chin and Jaw**: People with a small set of chin and jaws favor quality over quantity. They are sophisticated and prefer long-term relationships over episodic flings. Their approach to any subject can be quite conventional and "by the book." At the same time, they prefer to stick to their roots or traditions to ascertain their personal values.

· **Sharp or Prominent Chin and Jaw**: A sharp and chiseled jawline is immediately visible on one's face. These people like to be in charge at home and in the workplace. They are aware of their exceptional leadership qualities, which makes them deeply judgmental and opinionated. They are inherently strong and like to hold their ground. If they believe in something with all their heart, they will stand up and fight for it tooth and nail.

Hair

The color and texture of one's hair can reveal things about them as well. The most common hair colors are black, blond, brown, and ginger.

Traits Based on the Color of a Person's Hair

· **Black Hair:** People with black hair tend to be calmer than their counterparts. If the hair is straight, it means that the person is also melancholic. People with straight black hair seem to emit negative vibes around them. They are often pessimistic and cynical in their vision of life, but if they have black and curly hair, they may be more jolly, caring, and affectionate.

· **Blonde Hair:** These people are the most curious of the lot and have a phenomenal memory. Even if they are not physically weak, they may appear so at times, but compared to other hair types, these people are indeed often physically weak. They have a unique talent for making a good impression and can ease any situation. Even if they don't show it, they are often self-conscious. Lastly, they are obedient and show youthfulness through their cheerful nature.

· **Redheaded or Ginger Hair:** People with red hair may come across as angry and skeptical, always ready to argue or start a fight. They are also short-tempered, which makes it easy to trigger them. Their strong physical energy and brutality may be scary, which is why most people tend to avoid engaging with them.

· **Brown Hair:** Brown-haired individuals enjoy traveling and are always seen out on an adventure. They have personality and character, which makes them very charming and attractive. They can easily blend in with others but may offend some due to their outspokenness or dissident views. Although they are mostly liberal, they may be surprising at times. Lastly, they are avidly romantic and passionate in bed.

Examples

Here, we take a look at famous personalities to understand the Five Elements of face reading and their apparent traits:

1. Wood

Famous personalities: Former Japanese Prime Minister Junichiro Koizumi and former US President Barack Obama.

Prominent attributes based on the Wood element: The face type is usually oval or an inverted triangle with a slim profile and tall structure. The forehead is typically wider than the chin. In most cases, the forehead is broader. People with this element are often found in positions of authority and power, often higher than most entities.

Their bodies are not fleshy, and they have long limbs. They are blessed with literary aptitudes and high intelligence. They prefer to think and work mentally rather than physically.

2. Earth

Famous personalities: The leader of the 1890s Korean independence movement, Kim Gu.

Prominent attributes based on the Earth element: The most common characteristic of these individuals is a thick body along with a large nose and full lips. The tip of the nose, wings, and bridge are all wide and bulbous. These people are known for their diamond-shaped face. Their high cheekbones stand out among other features, which is why their forehead and chin look narrower than the middle part of their face. They are respected due to their credibility and outstanding social skills. One of their most valued traits is that they listen to understand, not to speak back or argue. Finally, they have a rather relaxed personality, which makes them approachable and easy to talk to.

3. Water

Famous personalities: South Korean politician Ahn Cheol-soo and famous South Korean singer PSY.

Prominent attributes based on the Water element: People with this element mostly display a round-shaped face with mildly pronounced features. Their body is plump. Even though most of them have a narrow forehead, there are always exceptions. Those with Earth as an element and wider foreheads tend to be ahead of others, especially as reformative leaders and high-profile politicians.

4. Fire

Famous personalities: Former gold medalist in women's weightlifting Jang Mi-ran, and famous Korean entertainer Kang Ho-dong.

Prominent attributes based on the Fire element: Just like the shape of a flame, these people are often fiery and cheerful. They have a bright aura and are extremely vibrant, as opposed to those with the wood element. Although they are cheerful and lively most of the time, they are more oriented towards conservatism. They are very strong and have impressive physical stamina and flexibility, making them distinguished athletes. They are also believed to be gifted with quick reflexes, a crucial attribute in any sport. These people are attracted to specific athletic categories such as weightlifting, martial arts, or wrestling.

5. Metal

Famous personalities: Chairman of Hyundai Motor Group Chung Mong-Koo, and acclaimed actor, fitness idol, and politician Arnold Schwarzenegger.

Prominent attributes based on the Metal element: The most prominent features in these people are a strong jawline and a well-defined face, which is mostly square or rectangular. Moreover, their nose and nose wings stand out and are the most visible features on their face. These people have excellent leadership skills and are known for their integrity and self-righteousness. They are highly competitive and like to dominate and be the best. They are fit to be public figures, politicians, or successful entrepreneurs.

These five elements are so prominent in Chinese history and ancient medicine that they are considered, to this day, an effective way to assess a patient's inner nature. In fact, certain types of diagnoses involving the five elements are still used in modern practice. Whenever a patient has undergone internal changes due to a health condition, Chinese doctors always made sure to note any changes in their facial attributes. This paved the way for face reading to become an integral part of diagnosis and patient assessment in Chinese medicine.

Because this approach is essentially holistic, it aligns with the principles of Chinese medicine. A patient is seen as a whole rather than targeting specific body parts that suffer from aches, pains, or other discomforts. This approach considers the patient's body, mind, and spirit to treat them and help them regain optimal health. Lastly, these five elements help doctors determine the important attributes that are in balance and those that are not. Together, these reasons are enough to explain the significance of the five elements of face reading in Chinese medicine.

By studying these five elements, you will gain a better understanding of people and their behavior. You will learn about yourself in both private and public settings and gain insights into others around you. It will help you deal with people sensibly and give you enough reaction time before judging a person. At the end of the day, everyone is unique, and each individual possesses a different set of strengths and weaknesses.

Chapter 4: Reading the Past, Present, and Future

A person's face can be analyzed to read their past, present, and future. It is based on the ancient Chinese face reading technique that divides human life in a cycle of 99 to 100 years, from a person's birth to their death. A specific facial feature represents each year. In other words, a person's 99 years, which is the full life cycle, are marked on the face. You can easily figure out their past, present, and future by spotting the year patches with their facial features. In this section, we will be analyzing each life phase and its corresponding facial feature.

Let's take a look at these stages with respect to the facial features they represent and what they say about the person.

1. 0 to 14 Years

Represented by: Ears.

The ears represent a person's childhood, from birth to fourteen years of age. If the ears are thick, fleshy, and well-defined, it means that the person is or has been blessed with a supportive entourage (family, friends) and great health during that time. While the left ear designates a person's early childhood, from birth to seven years of age, the right ear represents their late childhood, from eight to fourteen years of age. To predict a person's past during these years, take a look at the respective ear. If one has a scar, discoloration, or is shaped differently than the other ear, it means that they have endured a difficult life during that phase. If both ears are out of proportion or bear scars, they most likely had a troubled childhood.

2. 15 to 30 Years

Represented by: Upper forehead.

Learning more about a person's past starts with reading their forehead, as it tells a lot more than the ears can. The top of the forehead, which is also known as the celestial region, speaks a lot about someone's past. A person's childhood is always fated and is never the result of hard work or talent. In other words, the childhood phase is written when a person is born, and they will endure it the way it was meant to be. This is why the upper part of one's face is also known as the Heaven region, which indicates that our birth and childhood fates are already predestined.

If the forehead shows scars, marks, discoloration, or bumps, it could mean that the person has had a challenging childhood. The easiest way to predict a person's past or childhood is to analyze the skin tone in that area. If it is dull or patchy, it could mean that they had trouble in school, a poor academic record, an inability to make friends, or even poor health. They might have also faced issues with their relatives and siblings. On the other hand, a clear and smooth forehead indicates a happy and healthy childhood. They are also blessed with a supportive family, immense wealth, ancestral property, help and protection from their elders, and a comfortable lifestyle. As kids, they are driven, curious, and on the right path to fulfill their goals.

While the phase between fifteen and thirty years old does not exactly qualify as childhood, it explains the person's life during their adolescence or young adulthood. The ages of fifteen to nineteen, which are the teenage years, are considered late childhood, when people still live with their parents, whereas those aged twenty to thirty are considered young adults. Although their written fate still dictates their circumstances, they can write their own destiny with dedication, perseverance, and hard work.

3. 31 to 40 Years

Represented by: The forehead, eyebrows, and eyes.

Just like the skin tone of the upper forehead reveals a person's childhood and youth, the skin tone and condition of the entire forehead determines the person's adulthood and career. If the forehead is clear, smooth, and round, it indicates that the person will attract many opportunities and enjoy a good career boost early on. Eventually, they will succeed sooner than others. On the other hand, a dull skin color indicates that the person may have to or might have struggled to achieve success. In some cases, they may not even succeed during this phase.

In parallel, the eyebrows focus on a person's life between the ages of thirty-one and thirty-four. If the eyebrows are closely spaced or even joined, this represents the unapologetic nature of a person. They are unable to forgive easily and do not let things go and may hold grudges against people for a long time. If the eyebrows are slightly curved, well-defined, and firm, it means that the person is positive and cheerful. Thanks to this, they will attract and build valuable personal and professional relationships. If the same set of eyebrows are widely spaced and thick, the person may also accumulate a lot of wealth within this period. It also means that the person is destined to live longer.

If the eyebrows are thin, it points to a person's introverted nature. They are unable to make friends easily. However, if they do make friends, the bond is everlasting. They choose friends carefully – friends who turn into family. If you notice any form of discoloration near the person's eyebrows, it could mean that the person will face trouble in their career. It will prove very difficult for them to fulfill their work goals. At the same time, they may also face health issues. Lastly, if the eyebrows are well-defined and evenly shaped, this shows that the person is driven to collect wealth; they will work hard to achieve their goals and become rich.

To determine a person's past, present, or future between thirty-five and forty years of age, also take a look at their eyes. If the person has big, bright eyes, they will easily succeed in their career during these years. In contrast, if the eyes are small, sunken, or deep, it could foretell a major obstacle in their career throughout this period.

4. 41 to 50 Years

Represented by: Nose

The nose depicts a person's wealth between forty-one and fifty years of age. If the nose is streamlined, straight, and soft, it means that they are blessed with good luck in regard to their financial situation. They may accumulate wealth by working hard in their early years or by inheriting ancestral property. Even if the person failed to achieve their goals or earn money before the age of forty-one, this decade could be entirely different and life-changing for them. They are blessed in terms of amassing wealth, enjoying life, and living it on their own terms. This middle-age period is crucial to keep progressing career-wise and to start preparing for retirement. These individuals also dedicate enough time to determine their life choices and plan accordingly.

On the other hand, if one's nose is small, snubbed, sunken, it means that the person may face difficulty in facing their family due to never-ending arguments and fights. For these people, family conflicts are perpetual, which could also lead to wreckage in their relationships.

5. 51 to 55 Years

Represented by: Philtrum (the curved part between the nose and the upper lips).

If the philtrum is long and clear, the person is blessed with kids, grandkids, and a happy family. They are or will be successful in raising a family that is healthy and fulfilled. They will also be blessed in their twilight years. In fact, a clear and long philtrum is so valued that it is often considered a sign of prosperity. However, if the philtrum is short, narrow, or scarred, it may indicate trouble in raising a family. It also means that the person may not be blessed with many kids and grandkids. A shallow or scarred philtrum is often considered inauspicious.

Since the philtrum is known as the fertility and energy region, it depicts a person's luck and ability to have kids, along with the resources they have. It also tells you about a person's longevity. If the person has a short philtrum, it means that they could die early. On the other hand, if they have a long philtrum, it means that they will live longer. Lastly, if the philtrum is flat, the person may not be blessed with kids or suffer from weak physical strength and low energy.

6. 56 to 57 Years

Represented by: Nasolabial folds.

Nasolabial folds are the lines or creases that extend from the side of the nose and run down to the corners of the mouth. When a person laughs or smiles, these lines become more prominent. While the left nasolabial fold designates a person's fifth-sixth year, the right represents their fifty-seventh year. If the folds are well-defined, clear, deep, and extend to the corners of the mouth in a downward-sloping position, the person possesses immense leadership skills and authority. This makes them proficient bosses at this age. By the age of fifty-seven, a person will have acquired enough knowledge, wealth, and experience to lead a company, which is where their luck helps push them forward. Additionally, these people tend to be optimistic, cheerful, bright, and get respect from others. They are blessed with optimum health and are inspiring individuals.

If any of the nasolabial folds extend beyond the corners of the mouth, it signifies that the person may suffer from health issues, mainly related to stomach and digestive health. In some extreme cases, the person may also be anorexic, which could result in poor physical health. Other than this, if a person's nasolabial fold is not properly defined, it could mean that they possess weak leadership skills, which could make it difficult for them to be great leaders.

7. 58 to 59 Years

Represented by: Cheekbones.

The left cheekbone represents a person's fifty-eighth year, whereas the right one represents their fifty-ninth year. People with fleshy, plump, and round cheekbones are blessed with good luck and fortune during these late years. It means that the person may finally succeed in their career (depending on their retirement age) or prosper. If the cheekbones are flat and glossy, they are blessed and will receive protection from their loved ones. On the other hand, dull and sunken cheekbones can indicate a person's uneasiness and inability to feel peaceful. Even if they manage to achieve their goals and grow successful, they will often target ill-intentioned enemies. Their jealousy could destroy a person's career and effort. This could add to the feeling of uneasiness, making them overly stressed and restless.

A person's cheeks are also known as their love region, which determines a person's love of life and their romantic relationships. If someone has round and plump cheeks, it means that they will delve deep into their relationship, and love and admire their partner. If the cheeks are uneven or low, then the person may be involved in an affair that could eventually result in a break-up or divorce. Wrinkled cheeks are also unfavorable as they are a sign of unhappiness and reckless old age.

8. 60th Year

Represented by: Mouth and lips.

A person's mouth and lips enable them to communicate ideas, emotions, feelings, and information. They represent your maturity and display your thought process to others. Since wisdom and maturity come with age, the mouth is the sole representative of a person's sixtieth year. If the mouth and lips are rosy, thick, and point upwards when they smile, it means that they are blessed with a happy and peaceful life at this stage. They will have a loving family with happy and healthy members. It could also mean that the person will be blessed with tremendous profits by closing a business deal or inheriting or selling their ancestral property.

An upright mouth with slightly upturned corners is also favorable as it indicates a major gain, a joyful family, and peace of mind in the sixtieth year. Thin lips that droop down are not favored as they indicate an unfulfilling social life and family relations. It could also mean that the person is always prone to sadness and depression. You may find these people abusing due to their short temper and a rough, pessimistic perspective towards life. Due to this, they will often be living alone, without their partner or family. Others may despise or fear going near them.

9. 61 to 75 Years

Represented by: Chin.

The chin falls under the "Earth" section of the face, which denotes the person's after-years or old age. The period between sixty-one and seventy-five years old relates to retirement, enjoying free time, and savoring precious life moments. If a person has a round and prominent chin, it means that they are blessed with happiness and health in their retirement years. The most favored chin shape is round, plump, and fleshy as it indicates that the person will enjoy a comfortable and carefree old age. They will receive respect from their entourage, love from their spouse, and protection from their children.

On the other hand, a person with a short, fleshy, or pointed chin will most likely be unlucky in their old age. Those with scars, marks, or discoloration in this area will be unhappy and lonely due to the absence of valuable friends or their spouse. Likewise, if the small area around their chin is discolored, hued, or dark, it could also be a sign of loneliness and the absence of their spouse and children. In worst-case scenarios, the person may succumb due to food poisoning, drowning, or water-borne diseases. Needless to say, those are not the most revered ways for a life's end.

Practical Approach

This section will explore the points on one's face and help the reader understand how to read a spot to determine the subject's past, present, and future based on their age.

As you already know, the upper part of your face and your ears represent your childhood and early years, until you reach early youth. As you age, your face's age points move downwards and reach the bottom, which is when you turn old. By referring to this diagram, you can easily pinpoint the facial features relating to your current age.

If your age point is spotted on the left side, it means that you spend most of your time worrying about your career and work. In contrast, if the age point is spotted is at the center, it means that you are at a critical crossroads. Also, if you notice any discoloration or marks in this area, it means that you could face challenges soon. The best part about this exercise is that you will be aware of an issue beforehand, for which you can ready yourself and prepare accordingly. However, whether it pertains to relationships, career, or health, the type of problem is always unclear. For this, refer to the other ways and techniques to read a face, which we will explain later on.

Let's take a practical example to understand this in a clearer way. A birthmark or mole on any ear indicates that you may have faced issues during your childhood. Next, take a look at your forehead. Does it look flawed as far as its shape, size, and color? If yes, pay attention to your parents, as this may signal a grave health concern or relationship problems with them. On the other hand, it could also mean that you possessed a rebellious nature as a teenager. If that is the case, your relationship with your parents should be safe. If you were subjected to a lot of pampering in your childhood and adolescent years, you might have a broad or wide forehead.

As you age, if you notice that certain moles and marks on your face are disappearing or have changed over time, it means that your fate can or has, in fact, changed. Not everything is set in stone, and things can evolve spontaneously. This can be due to either your own luck or your continuous hard work and efforts. Also, if you have done good deeds or possess a pure soul, your earth luck may mingle with a positive aura to influence and change your heaven luck.

Chapter 5: Face Reading in Practice

This section includes different case studies of faces, complete with relevant diagrams for illustration. You will become familiar with a wide range of faces with different features or traits discussed throughout the book. Additionally, this chapter includes ways to read large facial signs and individual features and look at a person's face to dig into their past, present, and future. Lastly, you will also learn the character traits of a person, along with their health, wealth, children, and relationships in the present and future.

Reading Moles, Lines, and Wrinkles

Since lines, wrinkles, and moles on a face represent a person's luck, it is necessary to understand these elements' location, size, and color to be aware of their fate.

Reading Moles

Moles are dark or light spots on the face that vary in size, color, and location. Some also contain hair, a specificity we will discuss further. First, let's look at how the color, size, and location of the moles affect or tell a person's fate.

Color and Shape: Round moles, which are also raised, are considered the most favorable. The mole should be bright with a dark red or black shade. These colors were the most notable in ancient Chinese emperors, who were often considered the luckiest. However, you should still be careful with black moles on some areas of the face, as it could mean the opposite. Even if one has a black mole, these should be hidden and not prominent on the face. On the other hand, red moles should be clearly visible. Moles that are yellow, brown, or gray in color are generally regarded as inauspicious.

Hair on Moles: While hairy moles are despised due to their unsightliness, scientifically speaking, these are less likely to provoke cancer. According to ancient Chinese face reading, hairy moles signify good luck and longevity. The person is blessed with abundant wealth and success. They will have a smooth life, receive help and support from others, and enjoy constant prosperity. Hairy moles are also known as "landlord" moles, as the carrier is generally wealthy and respected in society. If you are a man with a hairy mole, do not be tempted to trim the hair; it may reverse these desirable effects. However, women with hairy moles can cut the hair that is visible on the surface.

Moles on the face of men and women carry different meanings and have varying spot designations. Let's have a closer look at the moles' different locations on a man's and woman's face and compare the outcomes.

Forehead

In Men: Moles on the upper part of the forehead indicate a man's relationship with his family. While the specific spot on the forehead matters for predictions, the mole's color should also be taken into account. If it is red, the man is more likely to excel in his career and strengthen his relationships. In contrast, if the mole is black in color, it could mean that the person is confident but lacks the ability to cooperate with his subordinates. Also, when it comes to profit, he may betray his friends.

In Women: Moles on a woman's forehead represent her luck and relationship with her family and partner. While certain spots imply a bad marriage or bad luck with her romantic partner, other spots may indicate a threat to childbirth.

Eyebrows, Eyes, Cheeks, and Nose

In Men: The main career spots in a man are the cheeks and eyebrows. Red moles are preferred over black ones because the former is known to represent a successful career. The men will be financially independent and able to spend without any worry. While some points around the eyebrows indicate evilness and ruthlessness in a man, others indicate that they are bad luck for their partners, children, and family.

In Women: The Property Balance, which is the area between the eyebrows and eyes, should not carry a mole as it could indicate a poor long-term relationship. It also means that the woman may encounter trouble in their marriage. Although they are believed to grant good luck to their husbands, they may suffer due to their partner's extramarital affairs.

Chin and Jaw

In Men: Moles on the upper lips are always promising signs. If a mole is spotted on a man's chin, important structures like the house, its foundation, and the terrain are a consideration. If the mole is prominent in this area, the man will get into a real estate deal to purchase a property or a piece of land. It also means that the man has good tastes and prefers the finer things in life.

In Women: Just like men, women are also lucky when they have a mole on their upper lip or chin. However, certain spots in this region are considered more serious when compared to other spots. If that is the case, the woman may suffer from serious health issues, mainly related to gynecology, or sometimes harassment from her peers or partner.

Lucky and Unlucky moles: As you know, some moles are considered lucky, whereas others are not. So, how does one distinguish between the two? Let's take a look at the individual spots on the face and consider the presence of moles there:

Moles on the Forehead

A mole on the forehead is largely considered inauspicious. If it sits right in the center of one's forehead, it could mean that the person suffers or will likely suffer from career setbacks. This is mainly due to a lack of cooperation with their colleagues or from dealing with an unpleasant and repressive boss.

Moles on Eyelashes

A mole on the eyelashes is a bad sign. Even though these are barely noticeable, prominent moles indicate the seriousness of one's life. Noticing a mole in this area hints that the person may suffer in their long-term relationship or married life. Also, it means that the person may be unpopular or unattractive to the opposite sex, which could make it even more difficult to find a partner. For women, a mole on the eyelashes could mean more serious health issues, especially the ones related to gynecology. Men with moles on eyelashes are also prone to health issues, particularly in the kidneys.

Moles on the Hairline

A mole on the hairline is considered auspicious. For this, the mole should be hidden beneath their hair. In fact, the less apparent it is, the better their luck is. Also, the mole should be black and shiny rather than light-colored and dull.

Moles on Eyebrows

A mole on one of the eyebrows is also considered auspicious. While they may not be clearly visible in thick or bushy eyebrows, you can easily discern them under thin eyebrows. If you have a mole on one of your eyebrows, chances are you are highly intelligent and an excellent student. You manage to earn good grades most of the time. You may be more inclined towards literature and have ambitious educational goals, like graduating with honors or from an Ivy League university. Men with moles on eyebrows are luckier than women, as they possess more leadership skills and tend to be more cooperative. They get along with their subordinates and manage to excel in their professional life.

Moles on the White Area of the Eye

This is a rare phenomenon, but some people do have light moles on the white part of the eye. Finding a mole there is often considered inauspicious. Although these people are luckier in other areas of their life, they may suffer a great deal when it comes to romantic involvement and long-term relationships. They are very loyal and faithful, yet their relationship often ends up in breakup or divorce despite these admirable traits.

Moles on and around the Nose

A mole on the wings, bridge, and tip of the nose is also considered auspicious. Since the nose represents a person's wealth and financial status, it could foretell a major financial loss. This is specifically targeted at people with moles on their nose bridge who would suffer from an unexpected monetary loss in their midlife. Also, a mole in this area could mean that the person may suffer from health issues affecting the lungs and respiratory system. Moles on the wings of the nose are highly unfavorable as well. A mole on the left-wing of the nose is unfavorable for men, whereas a mole on the right side is unfavorable for women. While the gentlemen are with a left-wing mole may be unable to make proper financial decisions, saving money will prove difficult for the ladies with a right-wing mole, leading both genders to a pitfall. Lastly, a mole on the nose tip signifies that a person makes poor choices or indulges in bad habits that could result in a failed long-term relationship or marriage, or pose a threat to their professional career.

Moles on Earlobes

A mole on the earlobe is considered highly auspicious. Since the earlobes represent a person's luck, moles in this area bring even better fortune. These people are not only kind, warm, and generous, but they have also been blessed with long life and a stable financial situation. Apart from the earlobe, it is also considered lucky to have a spot on the helix or inside the ear; while the former is linked to good education and high intelligence, the latter promises a long and prosperous life.

Moles on Cheeks

A mole on the cheeks is also an auspicious sign, especially for those who hold their career in high regard. A cheek mole indicates they are very cooperative with their subordinates and are exemplary in their work. Since they are also driven, a promotion or a raise may come their way sooner than anyone else. A mole on the cheek brings luck for men who are serious about their professional development. They work hard, are highly motivated, and possess remarkable leadership skills. They are also good-looking, respected, and popular among their peers. On the downside, they may suffer from poor management skills or have a troubled love life.

Moles on the Lips and Around the Mouth

If a person harbors a mole on their upper lip or on the corners of their mouth, they are considered very lucky. A mole near the lower lip corner suggests that the person may have rich tastes in food. They like to cook, eat gourmet meals, and have a penchant for the finer things in life. Despite their apparent materialism, their taste in clothes, cars, and other lifestyle items is praiseworthy. A mole on the upper lip, if shiny and black, indicates that the person will enjoy a life of pleasure and luxury. They are often geared towards opulence and first-class experiences, such as fine dining and wine tasting

Moles on the Middle of the Chin

While a mole on the chin is generally considered lucky, a colored spot right in the middle of the chin may be troublesome. It means that the person may have to endure constant life changes, making it rather difficult for them to adapt. Also, since they tend to rush their decisions, it only makes their situation worse. It can prove difficult for them to move to a new city or relocate, alone or with their family. A mole in this area also indicates health issues, chiefly related to the heart and cardiovascular system.

Reading Lines and Wrinkles

Lines and wrinkles on a person's face indicate differently. Let's explore the different spots for face wrinkles and lines and find out what these say about a person.

Forehead

If a person has several lines and wrinkles on their forehead, it means that they have endured a hard life with little gains and many struggles. It also suggests that the person has had a rough childhood with no love or support, poor education, and unhappiness. A forehead with three lines or less is considered the most favorable in face reading. If a person starts to develop forehead lines early on, it could indicate tough times ahead in their midlife or a failed marriage for women. However, for some men, it could also suggest that they will start their working career early. A person should always develop forehead lines after the age of thirty-five for women and forty for men.

Between Eyebrows

Also known as the ophryon, this region between the eyebrows indicates a person's luck based on their career and wealth. Those who have wrinkles between their eyebrows are often impatient and cannot tolerate their own actions. At the same time, they are overly stressed about their career. Women who have lines between their eyebrows typically look for a stable emotional life, whereas men want to own as much as they can through their hard work. However, men with wrinkles in this area do not face any struggle with women and are often sought out by them.

Crow's Feet

Crow's feet are lines that form around the outermost region of the eyes, a phenomenon that occurs naturally with age. These lines are part of a cluster and become more visible when the person smiles or laughs. Since this region is also related to the Marriage House mentioned earlier, it represents a person's matrimonial life and their luck with long-term relationships. Men who develop crow's feet early on are unable to sustain their married life and often fail at it. Women with crow's feet are somehow more condescending and often the victim of abuse in a marriage. Those who have vertical lines at the outer corners of their eyes are also likely to experience marriage problems.

Under-Eye Wrinkles

This spot is the Children's Palace. It depicts the morals, good deeds, and merits of a person throughout their life. If the undereye area has more than two sets of clear, glossy, and well-defined lines, it indicates that someone has done well for others. Due to this, these individuals are blessed and often highly regarded by others. They are also lucky in terms of offspring and have a long life. However, if the undereye area is void of wrinkles, sunken, or black, it means that the person was involved in bad deeds and could be unlucky when it comes to having and raising healthy children.

Bunny Lines

Located on the nose's starting point (the ridge between the eyes), bunny lines represent a person's physical and mental health. If a person suffers from poor digestive health or is under constant stress, their bunny lines will be more prominent. They are hard workers, extremely competent, and will not face any trouble in being promoted at work. On the other hand, having too many bunny lines suggests that the person will endure a failed marriage. In this case, one of the partners is often emotionally or sexually inactive. They also fail to show their love and support for their mothers, with whom they lack a deep emotional connection.

Wrinkles on the Nose Bridge

If a person has too many lines on the bridge of their nose, they may be suffering from recurring migraines. They put in a lot of hard work, which causes constant aches in that region. Lines on the nose bridge can either be a stack of horizontal wrinkles or manifest themselves in the form of a cross. In the former case, people may notice a change in their situation. If the lines are too prominent, they may notice significant or life-altering changes. Finally, a cross in that area indicates good health and a strong immune system.

Wrinkles on the Nose

These represent a person's wealth and prosperity. If the lines in this area are stacked vertically, it could indicate the person's inability to handle money matters properly. Also, people with this feature are constantly looking for new ways to earn money. If the nose is small and shows wrinkles, it could mean that the person lacks ambition and is not keen on building a solid career. Despite hard work and great efforts, they will often fail to achieve their goals. Any form of wrinkles on a person's nose represents their money management skills and their professional ambition (or lack thereof).

Wrinkles on Cheekbones

Lines on the cheekbones depict a person's capacity for labor and communication. Any kinds of wrinkles on the cheeks, vertical, horizontal, or mixed, are a warning sign indicating that the person is aware of their actions, words, and deeds. Regardless of how minor it may seem, a slip of the tongue may induce problems with their friends, relatives, or peers. If they don't stay low-key, they could lose their position, status, or power. So, even if the lines are not yet visible on your cheekbones, keep track of growing lines and wrinkles in that particular region. If you notice lines on your outer cheekbones, this indicates that you will need to work twice as hard to reach your goals.

Lines of Cheeks or Laugh Lines

As you already know, the lines beginning from the nose wings and extending to the corners of the mouth are known as laugh lines. These lines, which are also referred to as the cheek lines, nasolabial lines, or Fa Ling lines, are represented as the Assistant Palace and are clearly visible when a person is smiling, smirking, or laughing. They represent a person's order, power, and coordination. It tells whether the person can cooperate with others and work productively and in harmony. If a person has prominent, clear, and beautiful laugh lines, it is a sign that they are blessed with good fortune and a desirable career path. In contrast, broken or unclear laugh lines that show moles or scars are highly unfavorable.

Wrinkles at the Mouth Corner

Wrinkles or lines at the corners of the mouth are a bad omen, as these indicate loneliness, hard work without any gains, and sometimes even financial losses. While the bearer manages to attract success and reach their goals, they may suffer from unexpected losses along the way. Also, despite being blessed with long life, it is not always favorable. They may find themselves living alone during their old age, have bad luck, or face indifference from their entourage. They are not respected or valued in their old age, which can be demoralizing and heartbreaking. Now, if these lines are tiny or cut short, you should pay attention to your digestive health as this is often an indication of stomach issues. If the lines extend downward from the left corner of the mouth, it means that the person may suffer from liver or gallbladder ailments. Similar lines on the right side indicate issues with the spleen.

The Most Common Types of Wrinkles

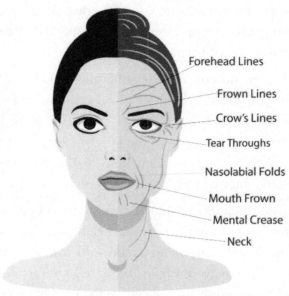

Forehead Lines
Frown Lines
Crow's Lines
Tear Throughs
Nasolabial Folds
Mouth Frown
Mental Crease
Neck

Reading Health

As you already know, facial features can be used to analyze a person's health. When you face certain health issues, your face acts as a map that can reveal worrying symptoms. For example, when you get jaundice, your eyes turn yellowish, which is a clear indication that something is wrong with your body. Likewise, even though they are harmless, moles often indicate potential health hazards in the future. If you notice a mole on your body, scrutinize it carefully. If it looks asymmetrical, even jagged, and seems to be growing, it might be the manifestation of an underlying health issue.

The same goes for other visible features such as scars, bumps, excessive facial hair, or pale skin. While these signs do indicate your current health condition, you can also use face mapping and face reading techniques to determine a person's state of health in the past and future. These reading techniques were widely used in the ancient

Chinese period for the purpose of diagnosis and assessment. As explained in one of the previous chapters, every point on your face is related to a specific organ. If any form of discoloration, scars, marks, or pimples appears on your face, it is a sign that the organ in question is under stress or out of balance.

While there is no concrete, scientifically-backed evidence behind face mapping for health, centuries of observation and research have led people to specific answers which cemented these beliefs. They also believe that the energy qi (or the flow of energy) is responsible for the inner organs' vitality. It is invisible to the naked eye but runs through defined internal pathways.

In the past, traditional Chinese health practitioners studied the facial features to examine a person's health. In fact, you can learn about the vital health points and features on your face and conduct a self-analysis. That way, you will be able to tell whether your organs are healthy just by contemplating yourself in the mirror.

Now, let's take a look at the points and features of the face to help us determine a person's state of health.

1. Forehead

Linked to: The stomach and digestive system.

If you notice any marks, scars, or discoloration on your forehead, it indicates an issue with your stomach or digestive health. These marks or scars are traditionally associated with conditions like irritable bowel syndrome and constipation. If you notice anything going on in the upper forehead, it is often due to your body's inability to break food down and the release of harmful toxins. The best way to remedy this is by detoxifying your body with a diet that's rich in antioxidants, including nutritious fruits and vegetables. Digestive enzymes and bitter herbs also work.

The lower forehead is often linked to the spirit and mind, meaning that any imperfection in this region may be due to mental health challenges. If your sleeping pattern is irregular and you are always under stress, you may notice acne, marks, or discoloration on your lower forehead. Adequate sleep is necessary to reduce marks and breakouts and limit stress, boost productivity, and keep you energized during the day. Make sure you rest at least seven-to-eight hours per night for optimal wellbeing. Other than this, practice meditation and journaling to keep your mental health balanced and in tiptop shape. Listing three things you are grateful for at the end of the day will release stress, make you happy, and give you inner peace. All in all, do whatever you can to maintain your mental health, as it could affect your face and skin negatively.

Traditional Chinese face-mapping techniques combined with modern-day dermatological studies and observations are used to determine health care and to diagnose and treat common health and skin issues. This approach was first launched by the American brand Dermalogica, which then spread widely in the cosmetic and dermatology industries.

Modern Face-Mapping Perception: The forehead is divided into Zones 1 and 3. Today, face mapping practitioners believe that signs and marks on the forehead are primarily caused by harmful dietary practices (too much fat, sugar, and salt). However, there is no concrete evidence or serious studies to support this claim. Another reason for breakouts, which is indirectly related to one's health, is poor hygiene. For example, if someone is not too careful in removing their makeup or rinsing off shampoo, it could cause congestion and block their pores. This often results in acne, which lends its name to the modern issue of "acne cosmetica".

Acne face-mapping is one of the most effective ways to target trigger points and assess specific health issues. This is done by examining and studying these acne breakout points in certain regions and prescribing adequate treatments. This is how most modern face reading practitioners diagnose health issues. With this method, you will not only treat your inner organs and become healthier, but you will also be able to prevent acne breakouts and replenish your skin.

2. Temple

Linked to: Bladder and kidneys.

Your temples are the areas between the forehead and the ears on each side of the face. Any issue with your kidneys or bladder can manifest itself in the form of acne, boils, inflammation, or infection on your temples. Also, if your body is finding it difficult to digest or is reacting to a new medical treatment, it is often apparent in the temple region.

Modern Face Mapping Perception: If a person's temples appear red or show any form of discoloration, it could be a sign of allergies or skin irritation. Low-quality makeup products, as well as their application and removal, are other common causes.

Face Mapping for Acne: The region around your temples may display excessive hair growth if not controlled. Apart from acne build-up resulting from bladder and kidney problems, the main reason is often improper makeup and shampoo removal. Pomade acne is a term used to describe acne breakouts caused by hair and cosmetic products.

3. Ears

Linked to: Kidneys.

While the symmetry, proportion, and location of the ears matter when it comes to face reading, they are often checked for marks or any form of discoloration to assess a person's state of health. If someone's ears show any form of discoloration, it could signify an issue with the kidneys.

Modern Face Mapping Perception: The ears are divided into Zones 4 and 10. In modern face mapping, ears that are red or hot is a major sign of unhealthy kidneys. The person should drink plenty of water to keep themselves hydrated. At the same time, they should avoid consuming alcohol or caffeine. Reducing salt intake can be beneficial as well. Improper makeup removal can cause clogged pores and acne on the forehead and cheeks. The ears may suffer from discomfort or redness due to excessive phone conversations, wearing headphones, or heavy jewelry.

4. Eyes (Particularly Under the Eyes)

Linked to: Imbalance in bodily fluids.

In the case of dehydration, chronic stress, or anxiety, your body will start to show puffiness, bagginess, or discoloration under your eyes. This can be easily treated by drinking more water and balancing your body fluids. Consume fruit juices and low-sugar energy drinks to adjust the mineral levels as well. To reduce dark circles and puffiness, use eye creams or apply cucumber slices. Also, try meditation to evacuate unnecessary stress and relax. Again, quality sleep is crucial.

Modern Face Mapping Perception: The eyes are divided into Zones 6 and 8. Other than an imbalance in body fluids, eyes are also believed to reflect a person's kidney health. Apart from dehydration, which is also the main cause of under-eye puffiness and dark circles, poor lymph flow and certain allergies are also plausible reasons.

5. Eyebrows

Linked to: Liver.

Since the liver is responsible for the detoxification process in your body, it is necessary to keep it healthy. Detoxification helps rid the body of harmful toxins and free radicals that could otherwise cause potential health threats. These also tend to increase body weight and should be flushed out. In case your liver is unhealthy, this will manifest as acne or marks in the space between your eyebrows. Detoxification is also a way to get rid of negative emotions and balance out mental health. The best way to keep your liver healthy is to consume superfoods that are rich in antioxidants, such as blueberries, green tea, and kale. Also, stay away from alcohol. Meditate, take some time off, and engage in your favorite hobbies to optimize your mental health.

Modern Face Mapping Perception: The eyebrows are divided into Zone 2. Modern practitioners believe that excessive acne breakouts may be a cause of lactose intolerance. Again, the main culprit is a bad or inadequate diet. By consuming fried, oily, and unhealthy foods in excess, your liver becomes overwhelmed and is unable to fulfill its detoxifying functions. As such, the best and simplest way to keep your liver healthy is to adopt a balanced diet composed of quality nutrients, including proteins, vitamins, minerals, and more. Cutting back on ultra-processed and caloric foods can also help restore your liver's health.

Face Mapping for Acne: Acne located on or between the eyebrows is often due to poor diet choices and excessive consumption of fatty, oily, and processed foods. So, as mentioned above, if you want to this region clear of any acne, limit your alcohol consumption and focus on a healthier, more sustainable lifestyle.

6. Cheeks

Linked to: Respiratory system, spleen, and stomach.

An even skin tone on your cheeks means that your respiratory system is in great shape. Redness, or any other form of discoloration in this area, is unfavorable as it suggests an issue with your stomach, mainly inflammation. Also, notice sudden breakouts on your cheeks or a sinus (an abnormal cavity caused by destroyed internal tissue). This could be the sign of an allergy affecting your respiratory system, stomach, or spleen.

Modern Face Mapping Perception: The cheeks are divided into Zone 5 and Zone 9. Nowadays, it is believed that the major cause of respiratory issues is poor lifestyle choices, such as smoking or vaping. This can cause hyperpigmentation around the area surrounding your cheeks. In parallel, poor hygiene, such as using a dirty cellphone or sleeping on unwashed pillowcases, can result in bacterial infections and acne. Improper makeup removal or the application of cosmetic products can also cause skin allergy. Another reason pertains to poor dental health; if someone suffers from tooth or gum related issues, this can cause noticeable changes in their cheeks.

Face Mapping for Acne: As mentioned, the main reasons for acne and excessive breakouts on cheeks are often a bad diet, dirty pillow covers, and unclean cell phones. So, the easiest way to avoid acne on the cheeks is to maintain food hygiene, regularly clean your pillow covers, and wipe your cellphone screen. Focus on a healthier diet and exercise a few times a week. Recently, excessive sugar and dairy intake have been established as potential reasons for face acne, specifically the cheeks area. As such, it is recommended to limit foods like white chocolate, candy and sweets, milk, yogurt, and cheese as much as possible.

7. Mouth and Lips

Linked to: Colon or stomach.

Among the facial features that are linked to the stomach, the mouth and lips comprise some of the most visible and obvious signs of stomach health. If you notice any boils, pimples, or ulcers on your lips or inside your mouth, it means that your stomach may have also developed ulcers. Also, if you consume a lot of cold or raw foods as part of your diet, your stomach may overwork itself to produce heat to metabolize the food and convert it into energy.

Modern Face Mapping Perception: The upper lip is divided into Zone 12A. The entire patch above your lips is directly linked to your reproductive health, just like the chin and jaws area. However, you may also notice some pigmentation or hyperpigmentation there caused by hormonal imbalances and melanin overproduction. When paired with excessive hair growth on your upper lip, a condition also known as hirsutism, you should get yourself checked for PCOS or PCOD.

8. Nose

Linked to: Heart.

The left side of the nose is linked to the left side of the heart, whereas the nose's right side is related to the right side of the heart. If you notice acne, boils, scars, blackheads, or excessive sebum or oil on your nose, it means that your heart may suffer from high cholesterol levels or irregular blood pressure. To keep your heart healthy, exercise every day for at least thirty to forty-five minutes to boost your cardiovascular health. Consume foods that are packed with healthy fats such as fish, olive oil, avocado, nuts, and berries. These items also contain Omega-3, a type of polyunsaturated fatty acid that's great for the heart and cardiovascular system.

Modern Face Mapping Perception: The nose is divided into Zone 7. Nowadays, experts believe that broken capillaries can result from a bad diet or poor hygiene. While changes in blood pressure and cholesterol levels may be more prevalent reasons, you cannot ignore the effects of pollution or pimple squeezing, which can cause acne breakouts. These may also be due to genetics. If you notice excessive redness, this may be a sign of high blood pressure.

9. Chin and Jaw

Linked to: Hormone production and the reproductive system.

If you notice any zits or sores on your chin and jaw, it indicates a change in hormonal levels. This phenomenon is notably apparent in women who undergo natural hormonal changes during their menstrual cycle. Also, if you notice excessive facial hair growth along with frequent hormonal imbalances, women should get themselves examined for reproductive health conditions such as PCOS or PCOD. If left untreated, it may negatively impact their reproductive system and the ability to have children. Excessive pimples on the chin and jaw also indicate mental health issues, such as stress, anxiety, or chronic depression.

Discoloration and breakout on the chin may also be related to gut health. Since your stomach and small intestines are represented by the chin, irregular bowel movements can cause acne in that area. Improve your diet and include more fiber-rich foods such as chia seeds, leafy greens, and rolled or steel-cut oats. Also, probiotics and fermented food promote healthy bacteria growth in your stomach, which is why kimchi, kombucha, yogurt, and sauerkraut can be immensely beneficial if included in your diet and consumed regularly.

Modern Face Mapping Perception: The chin is divided into Zone 12. Just like traditional practice, modern studies also hold that hormonal imbalances cause acne around this region. The center part of one's chin is often related to the small intestine. As a result, any form of food allergies, dietary changes, or unhealthy eating habits can result in acne in the middle part of your chin, which is why adopting a balanced, wholesome diet is of the essence.

The jawline is divided into Zones 11 and 13. Other than hormonal imbalances that can affect the chin and jawline, breakouts and scars in this area can also be due to poor dental hygiene. Since the jawline is linked to a woman's ovaries, they may suffer from excessive acne breakout during their monthly cycles. It can also be due to improper makeup removal that clogs pores; opt for non-comedogenic products instead.

Face Mapping for Acne: As mentioned above, the main reason for acne breakouts on a person's chin and jaws are hormonal imbalance, a claim that happens to be scientifically proven. If a woman's metabolism produces higher levels of male hormones or suffers from Polycystic Ovary Syndrome, she may end up with excessive acne. The only way to combat this issue is with regular physical exercise, a balanced diet, and weight loss if necessary. Hydration is also crucial, hence the importance of drinking at least eight glasses of water every day.

10. Neck

Linked to: Adrenal glands.

It is fair to say that the neck is not a central feature in face reading. Nevertheless, it can help determine the internal health of a person's body. Your neck is related to the health of your adrenal glands; when these are overworked and start releasing hormones, your neck and upper chest turn red. Adrenaline is one of those secreted hormones that pump you up and make you excited. Due to this, your neck becomes red. And while it is generally not a cause for concern, you should check for other conditions such as skin allergies, irritation, or sun damage.

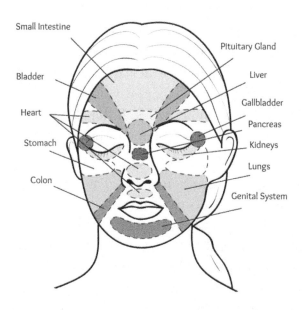

Facial Reflexology Chart

Use organic cosmetic products to prevent the appearance of boils, zits, or cysts. Also, drink plenty of water to keep yourself hydrated and even out your skin tone. More importantly, focus on your diet to promote digestive health. Lastly, make sure to get at least seven-to-eight hours of sleep each night to avoid stress and maintain both your physical and mental health. Exercise at least three to four days per week and aim for a daily meditation session of ten-to-fifteen minutes. Ultimately, a good diet, plenty of exercise, and small lifestyle changes will help you lead a healthier and more fulfilling life.

Consider These Signs as Indications of Possible Health Issues

· **Long Lashes:** While long lashes are often considered a sign of beauty, it can indicate an issue with one's eyes, particularly dryness. Your lashes should be one-third in proportion to your eyes. The cornea releases a certain amount of water, which is mainly controlled by your eyelashes. They also control the amount of air that flows in and out of your eyes and keep dust particles away. If a person has long lashes, the air circulation around their eyes increases, ultimately causing dryness.

· **Excessive or Deep Wrinkles:** Profound lines and wrinkles mean that the person may have a weak bone density, depending on their age. A modern explanation for this points to the early onset of menopause in women; as women age, their bones get weaker in density. This explains the relationship between deep wrinkles and low bone density.

· **Eyebrows and Weight Gain:** Thinning eyebrows, especially near the ends, are a sign of thyroid diseases. Despite being at a premature stage, you may suffer from a thyroid issue later on. So, if you also notice a sudden weight gain, it is advised to get tested for thyroid issues.

· **Crooked Teeth and Gum Disease:** From a purely scientific perspective, crooked teeth make food accumulate in the corners, which results in plaque build-up. Eventually, this could result in oral damages and gum disease.

· **Red Nose Tip:** A red nose tip is typically a sign of excessive stress. As the level of fire "chi" heightens, this causes complications such as high blood pressure, anxiety, and stress. If you experience a recurring red nose tip, you should get yourself checked for blood pressure issues.

These pointers are a combination of traditional face reading techniques and modern-day studies and findings.

Reading Wealth

Your face can reveal a lot about your wealth – your previous financial condition and what the future holds. In fact, modern face reading techniques mainly pertain to wealth. Mountains and rivers are significant symbols in terms of wealth and abundance, which is why it can be useful to consider these indicators while reading a face. Face reading experts begin from the central axis of the face and move in alternate directions to determine a person's wealth. Next, they examine the face's symmetry and balance to corroborate their initial readings. The more balance in symmetry and harmony, the more stability the person will have in their financial situation. Both of these aspects should be studied accurately to determine wealth.

Here is a breakdown of the "requirements" on one's face to assess their financial prospects:

1. First Wealth Spot – Symmetry Vital

This is the most crucial requirement when reading wealth. Both sides of your face should be symmetrical and possess a nice balance. On the one hand, if that is the case, your life and financial prospects will be smooth and indicative of stability and abundance. On the other hand, if the face lacks symmetry and balance, be prepared to endure a difficult life. As mentioned, to determine the symmetry of one's face, look at the central axis carefully. Both sides should be even. If your face shows perfect symmetry, you are considered extremely lucky. However, certain hairstyles may offset a person's facial symmetry, which could lead to an inaccurate reading. To avoid this, choose your hairstyle carefully; wear your hair in a way that does not cause disequilibrium.

2. Second Wealth Spot – Forehead High

As you already know, high and rounded foreheads are very favorable, especially when it comes to wealth. In fact, it is the second most accurate indicator of a financial situation. The forehead is represented by the prosperity mountain, which is a vital indicator of wealth. In the same way that mountains are high, round, gently curved, and a bit protruding, a forehead with these attributes is considered a sign of good fortune and financial prosperity. It also represents power, intellect, and authority.

An individual with a high forehead may also be blessed with abundant wealth at an early age. Since the forehead is located in the Heaven section, it is believed that people with high foreheads are blessed with wealth since birth. In other words, they are destined to live comfortably and have a lot of money. As mentioned, these people have authority over others and are blessed with a confident personality, which encourages other people to listen to them and seek their advice. However, these foreheads are quite rare. Even if someone has a mildly prominent forehead, they are still considered lucky and blessed financially. Besides this, the person possesses the ability to make quick decisions and is highly intelligent.

A perfect forehead is represented by the heavenly celestial dragon, an omen of great luck, power, and abundance. The reason for the area being the second-best indicator of luck and wealth owes to the fact that it is the spot of yang. Black moles located in the center of the forehead are rather unfavorable; that said, you can have them removed with professional help. However, if you spot any red moles on your forehead, they are believed to bring luck, so they are best left as is.

Taking care of your forehead to avoid pimples, acne, and blemishes is crucial. Wash your face in the morning and before bedtime, apply moisturizer, and use an organic scrub twice a week. If you have an oily T-zone, clean your face with a foam cleanser, and apply pore-cleansing masks. It is okay to use skincare products to keep the area clean, smooth, and blemish-free. You can also use cosmetics to keep the skin tone even and prevent the area from growing dull.

3. Third Wealth Spot – Money Nose

The third prominent wealth spot is the nose. Face reading experts examine the volume and size of the person's nose to determine their wealth. While a big nose may appear ugly and out of proportion on the face, it is still considered a lucky feature. It also indicates the person's money-making gateways or sources. It is believed that reading noses to determine wealth is more effective in women than in men. The rounder the nose, the luckier you are in terms of wealth and financial stability. The nostrils' size should also be factored in; average-sized nostrils (not too big, nor too small) are another sign of good fortune.

If a woman has a large, round, and high nose, she will attract wealth towards her and bring luck and wealth to the man she marries. However, accurate readings for wealth cannot be conducted on surgically altered noses as these are inauthentic and unnatural. As a general rule, a person's nose shouldn't be corrected for aesthetic purposes. It is believed that famous pop star Michael Jackson suffered a downward spiral and a tragic death after he underwent several rhinoplasties. The changes were drastic and transformed his face entirely.

With this said, artificial aids like makeup or skincare products can still be used to keep the nose smooth, spot-free, and shiny. Try to keep the nose clean, free of hair and blemishes, and to eliminate blackheads. Since spots, blemishes, discoloration, or scars on your nose are unfavorable, you need your nose bridge to be bright and luminous to experience an affluent and comfortable life.

Your nose is represented by one of the significant rivers that symbolize the face, which is the river Jie, famously known to depict wealth and prosperity. This spot is the third most crucial indicator of luck and wealth because it is the spot of yin. Just like the forehead, moles on noses, especially on the tip, are also unfavorable as these often signify bad luck.

So, the next time you notice your large nose in the mirror, do not feel self-conscious; be happy as you will be blessed with abundant wealth in the future.

4. Fourth Health Spot – Pearl Lip

Up next, another wealth indicator is the protrusion on top of one's lip, otherwise known as the Pearl Lip. If a person has a pearl lip, it means that they are fated to have abundant wealth and stable financial life. Pearls, as gemstones, are regarded as one of the most precious things in traditional Chinese philosophy and symbolize prestige and class. Also known as phoenix pearl, this feature represents a person's strong communication skills and highly developed speech.

Like the shape of a pearl, the protrusion above the lips looks round, a feature acquired at birth. It is apparent and visible on the person's upper lip right from a young age. In this case, it is safe to say that the child will be blessed with immense wealth in the future.

A pearl lip is not only favorable in terms of wealth but is also regarded as a characteristic of beauty. It is often compared to exotic features such as a dimple or a cleft chin, which makes a person attractive. This feature is often more prominent in women than in men. Even though it is considered a sign of luck for both genders, it is particularly appreciated and looked for in women. The reason for this is that females with a pearl mouth tend to bring luck, wealth, and prosperity to the men they marry.

5. Fifth Wealth Spot – Lotus Mouth

Aside from its shape and plumpness, the main factor that determines an attractive mouth is moisture. In this analysis, the mouth can be small in size; the only requirement is that your lips should be moist and shiny at all times. Your Lotus mouth is represented by one of the rivers that symbolize the face, namely the river Huai. It is the second most important one, despite it being smaller than other rivers. Now, since it is small, delicate, and succulent, this fifth wealth spot should portray the same features. Black moles on or around the mouth are highly unfavorable. You can choose to remove them with professional help. On the other hand, if you detect any red moles in that area, leave them alone as these are a sign of luck and indicate that you will never run out of food.

The name Lotus mouth derives from the flower that thrives in moist environments. This sign of abundant wealth and financial stability comes with a mouth and lips that are always moist. Just as a dry river is unfavorable, a dry mouth indicates poor luck in terms of wealth. So, do your best to keep your mouth and lips moist by applying lip balms and drinking plenty of water. Additionally, a bright red lipstick is also favored for women, as it is believed to bring good luck. Simultaneously, bright color on the lips is believed to attract yang chi, another highly favorable omen.

6. Sixth Wealth Spot – Strong Chin

The chin is represented by the base mountain and should ideally protrude to reproduce its shape. In this case, the person is blessed with great wealth, mainly with the help of physical assets. Along with the chin, a sharp and prominent jawline is also preferred. The chin should be fleshy and prominent as well. A shape that resembles a mountain is highly favored. Along with wealth and prosperity, a sharp and prominent chin also represents a person's longevity.

On the other hand, if you notice receding jawlines, it means that the person could face immense bad luck in their old age. In extreme cases, the person could also die a tragic and premature death.

7. Seventh Wealth Spot – Bright Eyes

Bright eyes are not just mesmerizing, but they can also depict a person's wealth and tell whether a person is alert and aware. While the shape and size of most facial features are considered to assess a person's luck and wealth, the vitality of the eyes is more relevant here. When it comes to determining wealth, the size, color, and position of one's eyes don't matter; what matters is their brightness. If your eyes are bright and possess a steady gaze, you are blessed with good fortune and abundant wealth.

The seventh spot is also measured by the eyebrows, which also act as an element of protection. If you have arched eyebrows that protect your bright eyes, it means that you are blessed with good health, wealth, and fortune. It is desirable to have thick and well-defined eyebrows. So, if you are thinking of shaving them for a new look, rethink your decision. A face devoid of eyebrows is considered undesirable. Even if you want to pluck your eyebrows, refrain from plucking them above the eyebrow line as it could affect your luck.

It is also believed that the eyebrows protect a person from jealous people's negative energy and ward off evil spirits. You can still use makeup such as eyebrow brushes and eyeliners to groom and shape your eyebrows and introduce symmetry between both eyes. Just like your face needs symmetry and balance for good luck, your eyes and eyebrows should be symmetrical as well.

8. Eighth Wealth Spot – Plump Cheekbones

The cheekbones fall under the Human section, which defines a person's midlife. When defining wealth, bright, smooth, and plump cheekbones are desirable. Additionally, if they are luminous and shiny, it indicates immense wealth in a person's life. Bony or thin cheekbones are highly undesirable as they symbolize yang energy, which is harmful.

If your cheekbones are fleshy, they may look tempting enough to pinch (you might have even experienced that a couple of times). Lastly, face reading experts also determine a person's wealth through the color or shade of their cheekbones. On the one hand, bright pink cheekbones indicate that the person is blessed with good fortune. On the other hand, dry, dull, colorless, or sunken cheekbones are unfavorable and suggest possible losses in the near future.

9. Ninth Wealth Spot – Ears

The ninth and final wealth spot is a pair of well-defined and positioned ears. This is represented by the Yellow River, also a symbol of good fortune. To measure a person's wealth, long ears are usually preferred over shorter ones as they depict class and prestige. Besides, since the Lord Buddha had long ears, they are more favored in traditional Chinese face reading. Along with the ears' proportion and position, Chinese face readers also examine whether the person's ears are fleshy, seeing as fleshy ears are more favorable.

You may have noticed that a majority of the wealth spots are located in the middle of the Human section, as everyone is responsible for changing their luck and attracting success through hard work and effort. The youth and old age section contain just a few wealth points because you will work hard to achieve your mid-life goals, meaning that your wealth points are well-defined by the time you grow old.

Fertility and Gender Prediction

Face reading is quite popular among couples who are trying to have a baby. It indicates a person's fertility and can help predict the gender of their baby.

1. Temple

Gender prediction for baby: If this region is bright, smooth, and free of any kind of discoloration, it indicates that the father may have a baby girl. The couple will not face any difficulty in conceiving a child. They will enjoy an effortless pregnancy journey. On the other hand, if you notice that this region is dark or scarred, the couple may have to endure a difficult pregnancy journey. It is also a sign of expecting a baby girl.

2. Eyes

Gender prediction for baby: The mother's eyes can say a lot about her baby's gender. If she has wrinkles near her eyelashes (measuring around four to seven millimeters in length), she may have a baby boy. However, if the woman has no wrinkles on or around her eyes, she may expect a baby girl.

3. Eyebrows

Gender prediction for baby: This is more evident in the eyebrows of the father. If he possesses long, well-defined, and shining eyebrows, the chances of having a boy is sixty percent or more. With the same set of eyebrows and harder hair texture, the odds increase to around eighty to ninety percent. If his eyebrows are thin, sparse, or short, he may have a girl. Likewise, the baby's gender can be predicted from the mother's eyebrows. If her left eyebrow is longer, she may have a baby boy; if her right eyebrow is longer, she may have a baby girl. Just like the father, if the mother's eyebrows are thin, sparse, or short, she may expect a baby girl.

4. Ears

Gender prediction for baby: One of the easiest ways to predict a baby's gender is by taking a closer look at the mother's ears and earlobes. If you notice the presence of large ear lobes on a mother, she is highly likely to have a boy. In contrast, an absence of earlobes could be a sign of a baby girl being born.

5. Lips

The color of a woman's lips relates to her fertility and helps predict her baby's gender. If the color is rich or normal, it means that the woman will have a higher chance of getting pregnant.

Gender prediction for baby: In parallel, the father's and mother's philtrum can determine their baby's gender. A man's left-inclined philtrum indicates a higher chance of having a baby boy, whereas a right-inclined philtrum indicates a baby girl. The amount of hair on the philtrum region is also a factor to consider in a man; if he barely has any, the father could have a baby girl. The color of the lips also reveals the gender of the baby. For instance, if the mother's lips are red, pink, or rosy, she may have a boy. On the other hand, if the color is blue, white, or deep red, she may have a girl.

6. Chin and Jaw

A round chin depicts a person's luck in having abundant wealth and healthy relationships and indicates that they will be blessed with having many children and grandchildren.

Gender prediction for baby: If the jaw is square-shaped and the chin round, it means that the person will have a baby boy. If the chin is pointed at the end, it means that the person will have a baby girl.

Reading your Relationships and Marriage

This section will discuss how facial features relate to the state of a relationship for men and women. Both genders need to have two or more of the following features to have a successful relationship or a long-term marriage.

In Women:

· She should have a broad nose that represents high confidence, self-awareness, and independence.

· If a woman has Phoenix Eyes, she is witty, elegant, and can easily attract men. She is also very classy, which is another attractive trait.

· A rounded and average-sized forehead (four or fewer fingers in height) means that the woman is intelligent enough to make wise decisions, especially when it comes to choosing her partner and getting into a long-term commitment.

· If she has slightly curved eyebrows, it means that she is gentle, caring, and is able to express sentiments and feelings.

· If the nose's bridge is high, the person is confident and believes in equality between both genders. As her partner, if you ever try to suppress her, it may result in a clash or a breakup.

· If the woman has balanced lips, meaning that both the upper and lower lip are proportionate and equal in size, the woman can show physical affection and is sexually active. She tends to satisfy her man in bed.

In Men:

· If a man has a broad and high nose, it means that he is extremely confident and self-aware. However, he should have no ridges or bumps on the nose.

· Just like a woman, if the man has proportionate lips, it indicates that they are capable of showing physical affection and are distinguished lovers, especially in bed.

· A set of thick and well-defined eyebrows on a man indicates that he cherishes his relationship, to the point of foregoing other important aspects of his life (work, social circle, etc.).

· A well-defined hairline that sits away from the temples (at least at a distance of two fingers' width) is a strong sign of respect and trust in a relationship. Both partners have a mutual sense of understanding and respect for each other. Neither partner controls the other or shows too much complacency, which indicates a solid and happy marriage.

· Lastly, if the man has a wide chin, it means that he enjoys spending time at home with his wife. Simple pleasures like cuddling, watching a movie, or cooking together are what he always looks forward to.

Late Marriage Implications

People who are not lucky enough to find a long-term partner at an early age, or choose to marry late, should also consider certain factors when reading facial features.

· **Bulging Forehead:** A bulging forehead is an apparent sign of late marriage for both men and women. Since the forehead is represented by the fire element among the five elements, the forehead's protrusion depicts the blazing fire form. These individuals seem to be irresolute and uncompromising, which often leads to late marriage. A man who marries a woman with a protruding head may suffer due to mental complications and stress. Apart from a protrusion, a high forehead is also a sign of late marriage. As mentioned, the forehead is represented as the fire sign, which is why people with a high forehead prefer to choose passively. They also show a great deal of patience and do not rush their decisions to find a partner or get married.

· **Thick or Thin Eyebrows:** Typically, people with thick eyebrows are overthinkers who are unable to narrow down their options. Even though they wish to marry early, their indecisive character stands in the way. On the other hand, if a person has thin eyebrows, the chances are that they favor their own convenience over that of others. They are also unmoved by emotions and are quite selective. It is also difficult for them to stay devoted or be serious in any kind of relationship, whether it is marriage, children, or family, which is why they usually marry later than others.

· **Thick and Straight Hair:** Ancient Chinese face readers believed that the denseness of one's hair is linked to the thickness of their blood. The denser the hair is, the later the person is likely to get married. It is mainly due to their inflexibility and lack of patience. Also, Yang's symbol is linked to hard and straight hair, which means that individuals with this feature may marry later than they anticipate.

· **Crow's Feet:** While crow's feet are acceptable or not generally a bad omen, too many lines are often a sign of late marriage. This is because crow's feet are related to a laborious life. These people take care of every aspect of their life on their own and never depend on others to get things done. This would explain why they are often stressed. Young people with crow's feet barely have any time to meet new people or cultivate their existing relationships due to their busy lives, which is why they often ignore marriage in their twenties or early thirties. Bright eyes with crow's feet are still preferable, as these depict a person's charm, popularity, and sense of humor.

· **Big Eyes**: Individuals with big eyes are often indecisive and anxious when it comes to making important life decisions. In light of this, they are unable to decide on their partner for a long-term commitment.

Potential Partners

It is believed that a person's facial features can also reveal a lot about the kind of partner they attract, in accordance with their own appearance. The features of men and women are different, which is why they attract different kinds of partners. Take a look at the traits of potential partners for each gender:

A person's Marriage Palace usually foretells their future partner's features. For example, if the Marriage Palace is plump, along with symmetrical and matching eyes and eyebrows, it means that they will have a beautiful or handsome spouse. On the other hand, if their Marriage Palace is sunken or their eyebrows and eyes are unmatching, it could indicate an unattractive partner. That is also the case with big eyes and small eyebrows, or small eyes and bushy eyebrows. Lastly, if the person has asymmetrical or ill-proportioned eyebrows and eyes, it means that their partner may look average or plain.

For Women: Curved and long eyebrows will attract a tall and slim partner for most women. In contrast, women with shorter eyebrows may marry a bulkier man. If a woman's eyebrows point upwards at the end, it is possible that she will marry a man with a round face and a short temper. She may get into fights or even be the target of constant abuse. That said, if her eyebrows face downwards, the woman may attract a man with an oval-shaped face and a good-willed and tranquil nature.

For Men: A man's nose, eyes, and eyebrows are often considered when determining their partner's looks. For instance, if a man has a well-proportioned nose that is rounder and straighter than others, he is likely to meet and marry a beautiful woman. Also, the nostrils should be unexposed. On the contrary, if the man has exposed nostrils, they may marry an average-looking woman. Men with long eyes and well-shaped, proportionate eyebrows will attract a beautiful woman, with whom they will enter a long-term relationship. Finally, men with ill-proportioned and dusky eyebrows may marry an average-looking woman.

While a partner's looks shouldn't prevail over their nature and compatibility, predicting your future partner's appearance can be a fun and entertaining exercise with facial reading.

Reading Character Traits for Children

Last but certainly not least, you can assess a child's character, strengths, and weaknesses by looking at their face and visible features. Even though you already know most of these traits, let's focus on the most obvious and important ones relevant to reading children's faces.

Using the Five Elements discussed early on is perhaps the simplest way to decipher a child's personality. Let's see what each element can say about them.

The Wood Child

These kids are extremely curious and always eager to learn and discover new things. They are intelligent and can often be found reading books. They will ask you "why?" in almost every sentence, and if they fail to get the answer, they keep at it until they do. Aside from refusing to take no for an answer, they tend to be highly adventurous. Their energetic attitude is refreshing, yet they can be difficult to tame. Take a leap with them and join them on an adventure to understand that life is not dull.

Prominent Features of the Wood Child

- A well-defined jaw
- A bulging brow bone
- A straight and well-delimited hairline
- A square or rectangular-shaped face
- Thick eyebrows

The Fire Child

Just as the flame of a fire is bright, vibrant, and unstable, a Fire child is always happy and cheerful, eager to spread their joy to others around them. They are full of energy and can hardly stay put. They are chirpy and often called chatterboxes due to their tendency to talk non-stop. The Fire child needs to be stimulated; if not, they may act up. These kids are highly sociable and like to hang out with their friends and meet new ones. Finally, they tend to be short-tempered and angry.

Prominent Features of the Fire Child

- Curly hair
- Bright and sparkly eyes
- Freckles and dimples
- Skinny arms
- A prominent or mild blush on their cheeks

The Earth Child

These kids are known to have a practical and methodical approach when handling projects, a surprising trait at such a young age. They are organized and prefer to finish important tasks before they have their fun. Even though they like to be with their friends and are sociable, they prefer not to be center-stage. They may not mind some limelight every now and then but tend to be quite modest and humble about it. They are emotional, fun, and loving people who are also loyal. However, they may be prone to jealousy. They need their friends to be sympathetic and understand them inside-out. If left alone, an Earth child may suffer from separation anxiety at times.

Prominent Features of the Earth Child

- A fleshy nose
- Thick or full lips
- A peach skin complexion with a yellow undertone
- Low cheekbones
- A round-shaped face

The Water Child

Just like the tranquility of a flowing river, a Water child is calm and serene as well. They often show a strong imagination and are highly creative. Even though they may seem like extroverts who share more than necessary, they prefer to keep the important things to themselves. They may only open up to the people they like and trust above all. They are intelligent, perceptive, and usually get good grades in school. At times, they can be a bit sensitive over trivial issues. Their energies vary according to their mood; they may be jumpy at one point or sensitive at another. During these times, controlling them can prove a very challenging task.

Prominent Features of the Water Child

- A rounded upper forehead
- A strong and pointed chin
- Large ears and earlobes
- Thick, long, and lustrous hair
- A nicely-shaped philtrum

The Metal Child

Finally, a child with a metal element knows how to stand their ground and act and speak in any situation. They can blend well in a group as well as play individually. You can call them "ambiverts." They like to learn new things and are always curious. If you want to make them happy on a special occasion, such as their birthday, opt for something simple, useful, yet modest, or ask them what they would like. This is because they tend to be reserved and do not like surprises. They prefer to have a steady routine, finish their homework on time, and enjoy enough stability in their academic and family life. They can be a bit stubborn, which can make it difficult to control them. However, these kids are extremely friendly, jolly, and lovable when presented in a public setting.

Prominent Features of the Metal Child

- Lower, sunken cheekbones
- A pale complexion
- High and long eyebrows
- A well-defined bone structure
- Prominent cheekbones

A kid's face and its corresponding elements are enough to determine their traits, strengths, weaknesses, past, present, and future. Knowing about your child can help you control them better and remedy the shortcomings early on to turn them into strengths. It is not only essential to make them better humans as they grow up, but it is also a major indicator of their happiness.

Conclusion

Ultimately, learning to read faces to understand a person's thought process, emotions, fortune, and the current situation can positively impact your understanding of them. You may start looking at people with a different point of view and take some time to decipher their circumstances before jumping to conclusions. With these techniques, you can make out the strengths and weaknesses of each individual and behave accordingly.

Whether it's a date or a potential employee's interview, you can easily figure out a person's character and their future by reading their face, giving you a heads up to make a wise choice.

Before you end this book, let's address a major question that most people face – Will plastic or cosmetic surgery of any kind affect the way faces are read? Even though we discussed this earlier, it is worth examining from a different angle. Face reading is mainly about who the person truly is, instead of relying on their superficial features and external facade. Even if you alter your face with cosmetic surgery, it will not change your inner self and the destiny you are born with.

Nevertheless, cosmetic surgery and alterations to your face may cause an issue with the people you are meeting, as they may have mixed feelings. You are presenting a new or different external self while feeling like the same person on the inside. Professional face readers may also give you a different or vague assessment, which is ultimately inaccurate. For example, if your ears are pointed outwards, it means that the person is a scholar and a non-conformist. However, if you do not like the look of your ears and try to hide or alter them through a medical procedure, this may indicate that you want to hide your non-conformist values from others.

We mentioned taking care of your face and eating healthy food to avoid acne, marks, and discoloration. This is because acne and excessive breakouts are a sign of poor health. By drinking more water, exercising, eating healthy, and using skincare or cosmetic products (not cosmetic surgery), you can certainly treat and remedy this condition effectively and permanently.

As our destinies unfold, our facial and physical attributes change accordingly. Since our facial features are symbolized by mountains and rivers, mainly for wealth, you must realize that these flatten and dry up at some point. For this reason, you should be careful and notice the changes occurring in your face throughout different stages of life. At the same time, it is crucial to take care of your face through natural and artificial means. While plastic surgery is not advised (as it alters one's look and results in an inaccurate reading and assessment), it is advised to use cosmetic products to keep your face clean and healthy and avoid pimples, scars, and discolorations.

Face reading is fun and gives you a sense of understanding about yourself and the important people in your life. In many ways, it can help you redirect your path and make significant changes to enjoy a better and more fulfilling future.

Now that you have a solid knowledge of reading faces, it is time to put it into action. Good luck!

Here's another book by Mari Silva that you might like

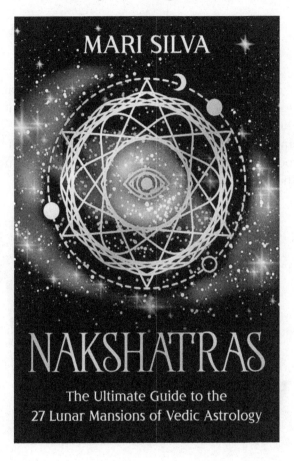

Your Free Gift (only available for a limited time)

Thanks for getting this book! If you want to learn more about various spirituality topics, then join Mari Silva's community and get a free guided meditation MP3 for awakening your third eye. This guided meditation mp3 is designed to open and strengthen ones third eye so you can experience a higher state of consciousness. Simply visit the link below the image to get started.

https://spiritualityspot.com/meditation

References

12 Houses Method of Face Reading, 12 Palaces, 12 Sections. (n.d.). Your Chinese Astrology. https://www.yourchineseastrology.com/face reading/12-houses/

Chinese Astrology: Chinese Zodiac Signs, 2020 Horoscope - YourChineseAstrology.com. (n.d.). Your Chinese Astrology. Retrieved from https://www.yourchineseastrology.com

Chinese Face Reading: What Your Face Says About Your Personality and Health. (2016, September 15). Conscious Lifestyle Magazine. https://www.consciouslifestylemag.com/chinese-face reading

Face Mapping: Can You Use It to Improve Your Skin's Health? (2019, August 1). Healthline. https://www.healthline.com/health/face-mapping#takeaway

Face Reading – Past, Present, Future - OHM Holistic Healings. (n.d.). Ohmhh.com. Retrieved from http://ohmhh.com/blog/2018/05/face reading

Foster, H. (n.d.). *What your face can tell you about your health.* Now To Love. Retrieved from https://www.nowtolove.co.nz/health/body/your-face-can-reveal-surprising-insight-into-your-health-36655

Johann Kaspar Lavater | Swiss writer. (n.d.). Encyclopedia Britannica. Retrieved from https://www.britannica.com/biography/Johann-Kaspar-Lavater

Mian Xiang - The Art of Face Reading. (2019, December 13). Beyond The Boundaries. https://www.btbmagazine.com/mian-xiang-the-art-of-face reading/

More Chinese face reading - 12 common face features and meanings. (n.d.). Picture Healer - Feng Shui, Craft & Art, Chinese Medicine. Retrieved from https://picturehealer.com/blog/more-chinese-face reading-12-common-face-features-and-meanings

Netmums. (2016, October 4). *What does your child's face reveal about their personality?* Netmums. https://www.netmums.com/child/what-does-your-childs-face-reveal-about-their-personality

Romance: Find true love through facial recognition | Relationships. (n.d.). Natural Health Magazine. Retrieved from https://www.naturalhealthmagazine.co.uk/relationships/face-facts

Src="https://Secure.gravatar.com/Avatar/A083c459bafb4053c71b98d05f0bdd8c?s=32, img C., d=mm, Hilton, r=g">Charlotte, Mar. 25, ersenUpdated, & 2020. (n.d.). *What Your Face Shape Could Be Saying About Your Personality.* Reader's Digest. Retrieved from https://www.rd.com/list/face-shape-personality/

Tsai, R. (2020, February 16). *How Does Face Mapping Relate to Your Health?* Beauty Within. https://beautywithinofficial.com/2020/02/16/what-is-face-mapping/

What Does Your Face Say About You? (2016, April 26). NaturalPath. https://naturalpath.net/mind/five-elements-face reading/

WOFS. (2006, September 5). *Are You Going Through a Difficult Time? Your Face Tells Your Age Luck - WOFS.com.* WOFS.com. https://www.wofs.com/are-you-going-through-a-difficult-time-your-face-tells-your-age-luck/

Made in the USA
Las Vegas, NV
18 April 2024

88811508R00075